HOOKED ON
Autographs

My favorite tales in collecting autographed golf balls from
golfers, entertainers, sports figures and U.S. presidents.
The stories will delight golfers and even non-golfers.

JOE GALIARDI

ISBN: 1-4392-3789-1
ISBN-13: 9781439237892
LCCN: 2009903817

Visit www.booksurge.com to order additional copies.

PRIVATE COLLECTION
OF GOLF BALL AUTOGRAPHS
OF
JOE GALIARDI

PRESIDENTS OF THE UNITED STATES

Richard M. Nixon

Gerald R. Ford

Jimmy E. Carter

Ronald W. Reagan

George H.W. Bush

William J. Clinton

Barack H. Obama

PROFESSIONAL GOLF ASSOCIATION (PGA)

Billy Andrade
George Archer
Paul Azinger
Seve Ballesteros*
Rich Beam
Notah Begay
Jay Don Blake
Tommy Bolt*
Chi C. Rodriguez*
M. Calcavecchia
Bob Charles*
Stewart Cink
Bobby Clampett
Jim Colbert
John Cook
Fred Couples
Ben Crenshaw*
John Daly
Chris DiMarco
Luke Donald
David Duval
Pete Dye*
Steve Elkington
Ernie Els
Nick Faldo*
Brad Faxton
Ray Floyd*
Fred Funk
Jim Furyk
Al Geiberger
Paddy Harrington
Jay Hass
Ben Hogan*

John Houston
David Howell
Hale Irwin*
Tony Jacklin*
Peter Jacobsen
Lee Jansen
Don January
Steve Jones
Tom Kite*
Bernard Langer*
David Leadbetter
Tom Lehman
Justin Leonard
Gene Littler*
Davis Love III
Andrew Magee
Casey Martin
Billy Mayfair
Scott McCarron
Gary McCord
Rocco Mediate
Phil Mickelson
Johnny Miller*
Gil Morgan
Byron Nelson*
Jack Nicklaus*
Frank Nobilo
Greg Norman*
Sean O'Hair
Mark O'Meara
Jose Olazabal*
Arnold Palmer*
Jesper Parnevik

Steve Pate
Corey Pavin
Kenny Perry
Gary Player*
Pat Perez
Nick Price*
Loren Roberts
Doug Sanders
Gene Sarazen*
Vijay Singh*
Jeff Sluman
Sam Snead*
Craig Stadler
Payne Stewart*
Dave Stockton
Curtis Strange*
Steve Strickler
Hal Sutton
Jim Thorpe
Lee Trevino*
Bob Tway
Ken Venturi
Scott Verblank
Lanny Wadkins*
Art Wall, Jr.
Bubba Watson
Tom Watson*
Mike Weir
Tom Weiskopf
Tiger Woods
Ian Woosnam
Fuzzy Zoeller

*Hall of Fame

LADIES PROFESSIONAL GOLF ASSOCIATION (LPGA)

Helen Alfredsson
Paula Creamer
Beth Daniels*
Natalie Gulbis
Betty Hicks

Julie Inkster*
Nancy Lopez*
Lorena Ochoa
Suzann Pettersen
Patty Sheehan*
A. Sorenstam*

Angela Stanford
Louise Suggs*
Karrie Webb*
Kathy Whitworth*
Mickey Wright*

BASEBALL

Ralph Branca
Joe Carter
Bob Feller*
Rollie Fingers*
Steve Garvey
Jason Giambi

Jeremy Giambi
Ralph Kiner*
Tony LaRussa
Kenny Lofton
Willie Mays*
Don Newcombe
Cal Ripken, Jr*

Brooks Robinson*
Bret Saberhagen
Bobby Thomson
Joe Torre
Matt Williams
Carl Yastrzemski*

FOOTBALL

Troy Aikman*
Marcus Allen*
Derek Anderson
Jerome Bettis
Fred Biletnikoff*
Terry Bradshaw*
Tom Brady
John Brodie
Jim Brown*
Bret Favre
Dan Fouts*

John Gagliardi*
Lou Holtz
Bo Jackson
Ronnie Lott*
Johnny Lujack
John Madden*
Dan Marino*
Joe Montana*
Joe Namath*
Jonathan Ogden
Jim Otto*
Joe Paterno*

Jim Plunkett
Jerry Rice*
Don Shula*
Vinny Testaverde
Joe Theismann
Y.A. Tittle*
Billy Joe Tolliver
Billy Wilson
Ray Wersching
Eric Wright
Steve Young*

TENNIS

Vijay Amritraj
Jimmy Connors*

Chris Evert*
Jack Kramer*
Rod Laver*

Pete Sampras*
Vic Seixas*

*Hall of Fame

BASKETBALL

Rick Barry*	Penny Hardaway	Michael Jordan*
Julius Erving*	Magic Johnson*	Antoine Walker

BOXING

Evander Holyfield* (four-time Heavyweight Champion of the World)
Leon Spinks (World Heavyweight Champion 1978)

ICE HOCKEY

Mario Lemieux* (Pittsburgh Penguins)
Luc Robitaille* (LA Kings)

SWIMMING

Michael Phelps
(Captured a record eight gold medals at the 2008 Beijing Olympics)

SPEED SKATING

Dan Jansen*
(Won a gold metal in the 1994 Winter Olympics)

ENTERTAINERS

Pat Boone	Harrison Ford	Regis Philbin
Glen Campbell	Sam Gatlin	Maury Povich
Sean Connery	Bob Hope*	Ray Romano
Alice Cooper	Samuel Jackson	Tommy Smothers
Kevin Costner	Jack Lemmon	Randy Travis
John Denver	Hal Linden	Jack Wagner
Clint Eastwood	Johnny Mathis	Robert Wagner
	Jack Nicholson	

OTHER CELEBRITIES

Keith Jackson	Donald Trump	Roz Savage
Stone Phillips	Elsie McLean	Chuck Yeager

*Hall of Fame

ABOUT THE AUTHOR

Born in Connellsville, Pennsylvania (fifty-five miles southeast of Pittsburgh), the author graduated from the Pennsylvania State University in 1957, where he lettered in tennis. Drafted into the U.S. Army following college, he spent the next two years stationed in Georgia and Kansas.

Upon return to civilian life in 1959, he was trained in public relations and advertising and worked for the largest independent bank in the state of Pennsylvania. In 1962, Wells Fargo Bank in San Francisco hired him to administer the bank's newly sponsored television show, *Science in Action*, a weekly half-hour evening program on KRON 4. He also handled public relations assignments for the eleventh largest bank in the United States.

In 1963, he joined Allstate Insurance Company in Menlo Park, California and in 1966 became the insurance company's public affairs manager in Sacramento, responsible for governmental affairs and PR duties. In 1968, he returned to Allstate's Northern California regional office in Menlo Park to resume the same duties. In 1993, after thirty years with the second-largest property and casualty insurer in the nation, the author retired.

He lives in Cupertino, California, with his wife Judy. They have two adult children and three granddaughters, Bianca, Caroline, and Hermione. Besides being a longtime collector of golf autographs, the author is an avid golfer and in his spare time enjoys reading, gardening, and renovating his home.

Joe Galiardi

DEDICATION

I dedicate this book to my loving wife and best friend Judy,
for her devotion and never-ending love for me.

IN MEMORY OF

Kathryn "Kitty" Galiardi
1933–1946
My sweet little sister Kitty, tragically drowned on August 5, 1946.
I think of her often. She will always live in my heart.

Kitty

IN SUPPORT OF

Walter Reed Society, Inc.
A percentage of the author's royalties will be donated to the Walter Reed Society, a tax-exempt charitable organization, established to, among other things, financially assist the returning severely wounded servicemen and women from Iraq and Afghanistan while they recuperate at the Walter Reed Army Medical Center in Washington, DC. The Society was founded in 1996.

ACKNOWLEDGMENTS

I have many people to thank.

To start with, I want to thank my very dear friends Travis and Barbara Poelle for encouraging me to write the book. Although the idea of writing a book about my golf autograph collection floated in and out of my brain, I didn't embark upon writing my very first book until Travis and Barbara firmly convinced me that I could do it.

I am enormously indebted to Susan Hafner for the excellent job she did on the copyediting for *Hooked on Golf.* I was so pleased with the way she smoothed out my text and was very impressed with her diligence in getting the job done. Her editorial wisdom and insight made it a better book.

I am also indebted to Richard Hoare, author, and former head of the English Department at a comprehensive school in England. He gets an A-plus for the fine job he did in proofreading my beginning submissions for grammatical and spelling errors.

Special thanks to LPGA pioneer Betty Hicks, who graciously agreed to let me interview her three times in her home. Her featured story in Chapter 4 is about the establishment of the Women's Professional Golf Association in 1944. Her personal memories of early life on the women's tour added immense value and entertainment to the book.

I also want to thank my good friends John Zasmuta and Alan Miller for bailing me out so many times when I encountered a computer problem while typing my manuscript. They know their stuff.

A special thank you to Nichole Murphy for her extraordinary work of photographing the golf room memorabilia for Chapter 15. She is an amazing photographer.

It's impossible to acknowledge everyone who at one time or another asked me how my book was coming along. I want to thank the gang, especially Lisa Poelle (Travis' mom), who read the book in various stages and gave me their invaluable advice and praise. Their constant encouragement gave me the moral support I needed to do the everyday legwork required to finish the book. Their friendship means everything to me.

I am grateful to all the professional golfers and famous celebrities who were generous to grant my autograph requests, especially golf legend Arnold Palmer. Not only did I obtain my first signed ball from the most popular golfer of all time, I also walked away with a personal experience that sparked my interest and launched my full-fledged hobby of collecting autographed golf balls.

As is often the case, there were others too who contributed to my collection, and I thank them. In particular, I want to thank Scott Somers, Head Golf Professional, Governor's Run Golf Club. I owe him a tremendous debt of gratitude for his generosity and support.

As part of my research, my periodical sources included *Golf Digest, Golf Magazine, GolfWorld, LINKS, R&A Golfers Handbook 2007,* and *NCGA GOLF.* In addition, I frequently used the Internet encyclopedia Wikipedia, to obtain and verify facts mentioned throughout the book. If I overlooked another source, I ask for their forgiveness.

Special thanks to the people at BookSurge for their guidance and creativity for bringing my mass of words to fruition. I could not have asked for a better team to work with and stay at my side to make certain everything went right.

Most of all, my deepest thanks for my loving wife Judy, my best friend and beloved soul mate, who coped with my long hours in the evenings as I labored patiently and mightily on the computer over the many versions (and I mean many) that preceded the final product. Judy had to make the supreme sacrifice of watching evening TV without her companion. Believe me, this book would not have been possible without her understanding and support that kept the ball rolling. I love her. But then, after twenty-six years of marriage, she already knows that.

CONTENTS

HOW I BECAME A COLLECTOR

At age seven, I already knew I was a collector. Indoors, shielded from the bitter Pennsylvania winter winds, I vividly remember spending countless hours in my warm and cozy cellar, building model World War II fighter airplanes, constructed from lightweight balsa wood and powered by rubber bands. I believe I owned the largest squadron of combat planes in town, by the end of the war, in 1945.

In the years that followed, I became a more serious collector. Delivering newspapers and setting up duckpins at the local bowling alley allowed me to save money that afforded my impressive comic book collection. My favorite comics were *Superman*, *Batman*, and *Captain Marvel*, easily read tales of good triumphing over evil. While I used my savings to purchase most of my comics, I also managed to win at marbles and pitching pennies. Skilled at these popular street games, I won many more comics to add to my collection.

At age thirteen, the Topps baseball card, bubble-gum era influenced my interest in collecting autographs. Despite living in Connellsville in Western Pennsylvania, known for its coal fields, my father dedicated his lifelong allegiance to the New York Giants, so that's where my love for baseball began. I could never understand why he rooted for the Giants instead of our very own Pittsburgh Pirates.

Dad taught me to appreciate the game, and like most thirteen-year-old boys who want to be just like their fathers, I never questioned his loyalties and became a die-hard Giants fan too. But like many teenagers, I took my enthusiasm to a higher level. I revered the Giants, studying all of their statistics, trades, injuries, and expectations for almost each player on the team.

When the Giants came to Pittsburgh, my father and I often visited Forbes Field to see them play against the Pirates, ignoring the angry scowls directed at us when the Giants executed a good play. We arrived early to the games to watch the batting and fielding practices. It was much easier to get players to sign baseball cards back in the late 1940s and early 1950s. In those days, the players were flattered when people asked them to sign an autograph. I would anxiously wait by the railing that separated the field and the first row of box seats, calling out to the players as they walked by. Eventually, I was able to get most of the Giants' signatures on my baseball cards, especially the big-name players like Willie Mays, Johnny Mize, Bobby Thomson, Sal Maglie, Larry Jansen, Alvin Dark, Eddie Stanky, and even Leo Durocher, the Giants' manager. I never passed up a chance to get autographs from opposing team players either, among them such Pittsburgh favorites as Ralph Kiner, Hank Greenberg, Bob Friend, Frankie Gustine, Danny Murtaugh, and Wally Westlake.

In the summer of 1947, I spent a month in Cleveland, Ohio, where I attended countless Cleveland Indians games at Cleveland's Municipal Stadium. Back then, kids twelve and under were admitted free. Again, I came home with an impressive collection of baseball cards signed by Bob Feller, Larry Doby, Bob Lemon, Al Rosen, and anyone I could encourage to press pen to card.

In the good old days, "Please, mister, can I have your autograph?" was all it took to get a ballplayer to sign his "John Hancock."

During my teenage years, when I was most active in sports, I collected baseball autographs. It became quite natural for me to resume collecting when I began to play golf in my later years. By 1986, I took up golf regularly after moving to Rancho Deep Cliff, a gated community in the foothills of Cupertino, California, where the mild weather offers ample year-round play. Rancho Deep Cliff is located next to one of the finest eighteen-hole executive golf courses in Northern California. It didn't take me long to become hooked on the sport, and my collector's nature led me into a new hobby: collecting logo golf balls from all the golf courses where I played. Not surprisingly, my first logo golf ball came from the Deep Cliff course.

As I played courses through the years, my logo ball collection developed, along with my swing. At one point, I needed to buy an oak rack to display the balls. The rack held seventy-two balls. As word got around about my new hobby, I began receiving logo balls from courses all over the world, compliments of my thoughtful friends. Within a year, the rack was full, and I bought a second one. When the second rack was full, I resolved to stop collecting logo golf balls and venture into something different: collecting autographed golf balls, pictures, and books. I imagined that my latest passion would prove to be more challenging, exciting, and fun. I also realized that it would enable me to meet a variety of famous professional golfers and big-time celebrities.

At the outset of my golf-collecting days, I made it an unspoken policy to never buy an autographed golf ball or sell one from my collection. I wanted the challenge of obtaining autographs from famous golfers and other celebrities by myself, for the pure pleasure of the hunt and the accomplishment. I'm proud to say that I've stuck to that policy, although I must admit I was tempted on a few occasions to buy on eBay autographed golf balls from well-known golfers who had previously turned down my request for their autographs. Luckily, not too many pros refused me. I changed the minds of some who initially said no by using a few tricks of the trade, which I later reveal in Chapter 14.

Truthfully, I didn't acquire all of my autographed golf balls personally, although I certainly wish I had. Although I obtained most of the autographs by myself, I acquired some through friends, by mail, and by trading duplicate balls with fellow members of the Golf Collectors Society, among other reputable collectors.

Hooked on Autographs shares my passion, as it details the behind-the-scenes struggles of collecting autographs from a parade of best-loved golfers, famous entertainers, notable sports figures, and even U.S. presidents. These pages bring together their personalities, career highlights, anecdotes, and famous quotes. These captivating stories should delight golfers and non-golfers alike. In a chapter called "Tricks of the Trade," I give practical advice and tips on buying and collecting autographs, based on my twenty-plus years of experience.

My inspiration for collecting stems from a variety of memories, but one always remembers his first. When, where, and from whom did I obtain my first autograph on a golf ball? Read on to embark with me on this proud moment. The first autograph came from a golf legend that did more for golf than any other person in the history of the sport. Known for swinging hard and finishing with a gyrating follow-through, this PGA Tour icon became a national folk hero with his late charges to pull off many victories. More than any other golfer, he receives credit for introducing the game of golf to the common person. Now that I have practically identified him, I'm sure you'll agree with me that this special and charismatic person deserves top billing.

It often takes much patience and perseverance to get a golf ball signed, an adventure I relate in Chapter 3. The individual I was after was a legendary movie star. I just had to have his autograph in my collection, and I never gave up trying to get this Oscar-winning actor's signature. I finally obtained it at Pebble Beach—a sweet day in a collector's life. You're probably assuming it was Hollywood legend Clint Eastwood. Good guess, but wrong answer! Indeed, Clint Eastwood is an Oscar-winning actor, but I was able to get his autograph on a golf ball at Pebble Beach's practice putting green. As he signed the ball, a flicker of a smile crossed his famously craggy face. "Dirty Harry" certainly made my day! The story behind how I was able to get this other actor's autograph is also a great one. I've told the tale many times to friends who have visited my golf room, and now I'm eager and excited to share the story with you in Chapter 3.

In reviewing the roster of my private collection of golf ball autographs that totals 221 at print time, you will notice many recognizable names and some that are not so well known. Chi Chi Rodriguez is practically a household name in golf. So is Lee Trevino. But who is Betty Hicks? Hicks is one of the pioneers in women's golf. She played golf at a time when women's professional golf didn't yet exist. Betty Hicks helped lay the foundation for the current Ladies Professional Golf Association (LPGA), and Chapter 4 is devoted to her incredible story.

You won't want to miss reading what happened when I went to interview Betty at her condo in Cupertino. The hilarious incident leads into her personal and fascinating account of how women's professional golf began. Her tales of playing during World War II fund-raising exhibitions with Bob Hope, Bing Crosby, and Joe Louis, heavyweight-boxing champion of the world, are sure to entertain and amuse you.

Another name you probably won't recognize is Elsie McLean. She made the *Guinness World Records* in 2007, and Chapter 10 reveals how this woman gained worldwide fame overnight with one incredible swing.

Because he was surrounded by his retinue of Secret Service agents, it was no easy task getting the forty-first president of the United States to sign a golf ball at Pebble Beach. Quick thinking on my part and having an "ace up my sleeve," as related in Chapter 8, enabled me to add George H. W. Bush's name to my roster of signed balls.

In Chapter 15, I invite you into my golf room, which has the look and feel of a golf museum. I'll guide you through an exclusive pictorial tour of my private collection of autographs on balls, pictures, and books. I have spent over twenty years amassing my extensive collection. Here, you'll get the fascinating stories behind many of the treasured pieces in the room, such as legend Jack Nicklaus playing his last Open at St. Andrews in 2005.

I hope you'll enjoy this account of my trials and triumphs in collecting autographs on golf balls. Every autographed golf ball in my private collection has a story to tell, and I bring my favorite and most memorable ones together in these pages.

Hooked on Autographs is a one-of-a-kind book. Until now, there has never been a golf book published about one person's all-out passion to collect famous autographs on golf balls and relate the fascinating and humorous stories behind the widely known signatures.

I hope you enjoy the book as much as I've enjoyed writing it. It's been a labor of love. I'm as enthusiastic today in pursuing my hobby as I was when I obtained my first autographed ball on October 25, 1989, at Silverado Country Club in Napa, California. That day marked a turning point in my life.

Joe Galiardi
email: joe@hookedonautographs.com

CHAPTER 1

THE KING

"I never quit trying. I never felt that I didn't have a chance to win."

My collection begins with the most beloved professional golfer in the history of the sport, Arnold Palmer. Arnie was the first star of the television sports age that began in the 1950s. His athletic skills popularized the game in the late 1950s and early 1960s and mesmerized viewers with his go-for-broke style and string of exciting finishes. His first PGA victory came in the 1955 Canadian Open. Arnie finished his career with sixty-two PGA Tour wins and amassed ninety-six championships in national and international play. Later in his career, Palmer helped put the fifty-and-over Senior Professional Golf Association Tour on the map, winning ten events. Arnie officially retired from PGA tournament golf on October 13, 2006.

Palmer has the distinction of winning seven major tournaments: the Masters, four remarkable times; the British Open twice; and the U.S. Open in 1960, the year he cemented his legacy. He won awards that year for both the Hickok Athlete of the Year and *Sports Illustrated* Sportsman of the Year. Furman Bisher's book, *The Birth of a Legend: Arnold Palmer's Golden Year, 1960* focuses on Arnie's explosion into legendary status on the golf scene in 1960.

Here's a look at some of his more notable firsts and record-breaking feats.

He was the first golfer to win the combination of the U.S. Amateur (1954), U.S. Open (1960), and the U.S. Senior Open (1981).

He was the first golfer to win the Masters four times (1958, 1960, 1962, and 1964).

He holds the record for the most consecutive starts in the Masters (fifty).

He was the first player to earn $1 million in official prize money during his career on the PGA Tour.

At the 2001 Bob Hope Chrysler Classic, Arnie shot a 71 to equal his age, becoming the oldest player to shoot his age on the PGA Tour.

He was the first golfer to be named Sportsman of the Year by *Sports Illustrated.*

He holds the record for the U.S. side for the most Ryder Cup match victories with twenty-two.

He won the first Palm Springs Desert Golf Classic in 1960, a tournament now known as the Bob Hope Chrysler Classic.

Arnie's legacy extends far beyond the golf course. He has devoted much of his time and money to support and promote charitable organizations, including the Arnold Palmer Hospital for Women and Children in Orlando, Florida. During the first of his four wins at the Masters in 1958 at Augusta National, a group of soldier volunteers stationed at Fort Gordon in Augusta strolled along the fairways, carrying signs that urged Arnie to win his first Masters. Dubbed "Arnie's Army," a legion of dedicated fans didn't simply cheer for him on the golf course as they have in the past; they've joined him in the battle against prostate cancer. The most common non-skin cancer and second-leading cancer killer among men, prostate cancer killed an estimated 28,660 American men in 2008. Arnie's Army aims to eliminate prostate cancer through education and by engaging local communities in conquering this dreadful disease. The general himself commands the fund-raising closest-to-the-pin contests scheduled in golf clubs throughout the country. These yearly contests have raised millions in the fight against prostate cancer.

Of the many books written by Arnold Palmer, I'm fortunate to have eight, all personally signed by the man known affectionately as "The King." I stumbled unknowingly upon his first book, *Arnold Palmer's Golf Book, "Hit It Hard!"* in a used book store in Murphys, California, a Gold Rush era town in the heart of the Sierra Nevada Mountains. Trusting that he would reply, I sent the first edition book, printed in 1961, to Arnie for his signature. Along with the book, I mailed a picture of him and Jack Nicklaus shaking hands at the coveted green jacket ceremony in 1964, when Arnie recaptured the Masters trophy from Jack. Not only did Arnie autograph the book and picture, he also sent a very thoughtful letter.

January 22, 1998

Dear Joe:

I certainly was pleased to receive and read your nice letter. It's always great to hear from people who appreciate the game of golf and it was my pleasure to autograph your book and picture. In your letter you asked me about the first book I had written to start your collection of golf books. It was "Hit It Hard" and was written in 1961.
Good luck with your new hobby!

Best regards,
Arnold Palmer (signed)

In 2004, my daughter gave me a special Christmas gift, Arnie's latest book, *Arnold Palmer: Memories, Stories, and Memorabilia from a Life On and Off the Course.* It relates the complete story of Arnie's life from the time, as he put it, "I was old enough to accompany Pap to the Latrobe Country Club, where he was the greenkeeper." The book, in an unusual publishing move, included Arnie's favorite pieces of memorabilia that were removable, like the "Arnie's Army" button. I'm grateful to Arnie for signing my copy, which is on display in my golf room.

Not surprisingly, when I decided to start collecting autographs on golf balls, I wanted Arnie's signature first.

In 1989, I learned that Arnie planned to play in the inaugural Transamerica Senior Golf Tournament at picturesque Silverado Country Club in Napa, California. I drove to Silverado Country Club on a practice-round day in October to see Arnie and hopefully get my first signed golf ball by the golf legend. My anticipation grew as I drove through the rolling hills of Napa Valley's wine country. I finally arrived at the breathtaking Silverado Resort, thrilled to see Arnold Palmer for the first time in person, practicing on the resort's putting green near knickers-clad Billy Casper, another famous golfer. In seventh heaven, I stood close to Arnie and watched him tee off on Hole No. 1 on the South Course. I eagerly followed his charismatic figure for the first nine holes and caught up with him again on the finishing hole. Watching him tee off on No. 18, a five-hundred-yard, par-5, dogleg left, with compressed trees on either side, I stood in awe as Arnie blistered his drive about 290 yards, drawing it around the corner. I don't know which club he used to hit his second spectacular shot, but it turned out to be the right choice, as the ball sailed over the bunkers in front of the green and landed at the back left of the long and undulating green. About twenty-five feet from the pin, he drained the putt for an incredible eagle-three. If that putt had won him the tournament during his prime time, Arnie would have tossed his visor in the air, as he did many times in winning past events. Instead, Arnie flashed a big, contagious grin as the large gallery erupted wildly after he holed the putt.

As Arnie walked off the eighteenth green, a large crowd of fans and autograph seekers buzzed with anticipation to see Arnie up close and get his autograph, with me among them. With ball and Sharpie pen in hand, I approached Arnie with a combination of glee and apprehension. Gleeful, because I was about to meet one of the greatest golfers of all time and nervous because I heard that some pro golfers don't sign golf balls. Arnie wasted no time and immediately started signing. When my turn came, he graciously signed. It was that easy! I thanked him and walked away, grasping my prized autograph with a huge smile on my face. I was absolutely thrilled to get my first autographed golf ball. It was not the last time I saw him in person, and with that autograph, I had launched my fascinating new hobby. I did not realize then that my private autographed golf ball collection would grow to become one of the largest in the United States.

Much has been written about the No.1 goodwill ambassador for the game of golf. Arnie hasn't been given enough credit for his willingness to sign stacks of golf items arriving daily at his native summer home in Latrobe, Pennsylvania, or at his winter residence at Bay Hill Club in Orlando, Florida. He signs every item the right way—very neatly and legibly. He was quoted in the *San Jose Mercury* as commenting, "I don't know where a player comes off, a young player particularly, asked to give an autograph and he scribbles something down that you can't read. Who in the hell knows what it is? Why take the time to do it? Why not make it legible?" In my case alone, Arnie has beautifully signed twenty items in my golf room—eight books, eight photographs, a golf ball, an old Arnold Palmer signature Bulls Eye putter, and the premier issue of the now defunct *Senior*

Golfer Magazine (June/July 1993) with his smiling face on the cover. The magazine is now a collector's piece, especially my copy, since The King signed on the cover. The most recent item added to my collection is the 2009 Bob Hope Chrysler Classic Fiftieth Anniversary program, signed by host Arnold Palmer.

Author and The King strike a pose at the Fiftieth Bob Hope Classic

At the PGA West Golf Course in La Quinta, California, in 1995, the Liberty Mutual Legends of Golf tournament took place at the Stadium Course, designed by Pete Dye and considered one of the most challenging courses in America. I eagerly watched many of the golf legends of yesterday, Arnold Palmer, Sam Snead, Tommy Bolt, Art Wall, Jr., and Gene Littler, to name just a few. Sam, Tommy, Art, and Gene graciously signed balls for my collection.

Later in the day, I sat down on a grassy mound with five other unknown spectators to watch some of the other golf legends tee off at one of the holes. As we were anxiously waiting for the next group of players to appear, Arnold Palmer and his caddy walked toward my group. While the other players in his threesome headed for the tee, Arnie did something unique for professional golfers. He came over to the six of us, shook our hands, and thanked us for being at the tournament to support the players. Impressed with his warmth and flattered by his down-to-earth thoughtfulness, I realized that his sense of caring and attention to the fans has endeared Arnold Palmer to millions of golfers throughout the world.

Why can't today's players be more like Arnold Palmer when it comes to making the fans feel welcome like he did for me that day in 1995? At the 2007 Arnold Palmer Invitational, Arnie was asked this question by commentator Jimmy Roberts. "What would you like modern players to do more of?" Arnie replied, "I would like to see the players relate more to the galleries. That would be a wonderful thing for the tour and the players. To lighten up a little wouldn't hurt at all." PGA Tour players, take heed!

Everyone who has ever had a tee time with The King has a story to tell. Here's one of my favorites. The final round of the 1964 Masters found Arnie considering making history by breaking legend Ben Hogan's 72-hole record of 274 and becoming the first player to score all four rounds in the 60s. On the par-5, fifteenth hole, Arnie crushed his tee shot. He decided to go for the green in two (his style of play), but he had to hit over the water. With the sun glaring in his eyes, Arnie could not determine if his second shot cleared the water. He asked his playing partner, the late Dave Marr, if his ball made it over the hazard. Dave said, "Hell, Arnold, your divot went over!" The tournament turned out to be a one-horse race, with Arnie winning his fourth green jacket by six strokes, shooting two under par 70 for a 276 total, thus becoming the first player to win the Masters four times.

Sportswriter Jeff Williams, in a 2005 article entitled "Coming Up Aces," described Arnie's holes in one at the TPC at Avenel in Potomac, Maryland. In 1986, Palmer aced the third hole, witnessed by a large gallery. When he arrived the next day to play the same hole, he informed the TV camera crew that they were a day late. Unbelievably, Palmer holed his second straight 5-iron on the par-3 hole, caught on camera and aired as the TV channel's news highlight that evening.

Comedian Tom Dreesen, the host of the 2009 Bob Hope Chrysler Classic gala ball, relayed a story about Palmer's character. At a major heading to the eighteenth tee with a two-stroke lead, Arnie played aggressively and triple-bogeyed the hole, losing by a stroke. "The average pro might have gone into the locker room and smashed things around, ignored the press, and stormed out of there early," Dreesen said. "Not Arnie. When the sun went down and all the players, caddies, and volunteers left the grounds, Arnie was in the parking lot signing autographs for little kids and their fathers."

Chi Chi Rodriguez has credited Arnie's affability for making golf so popular. "People on tour used to complain that Arnold Palmer got preferential treatment. I'd ask them, do you want preferential treatment too? Then start treating everyone the way Arnold Palmer does."

Legendary Gary Player showed the utmost respect for Arnold Palmer. On record, he said, "He gave of himself. If you give to the fans, they give back. Lots of athletes are aloof. But Arnold was always aware of the man in the street."

Jack Nicklaus, arguably the greatest golfer of all time, summed up Arnie's golf contribution by remarking, "Arnold is the reason golf enjoys the popularity it does today. He made golf attractive to the television-viewing public. There has never been anyone like him before in the game of golf, and there probably won't be another like him again."

There will be only one Arnold Palmer. The King and golf are linked forever. No golfer has ever been his rival. All who play the wonderful game of golf should be eternally grateful to this living legend for being partially responsible for the golf boom in the latter half of the twentieth century and paving the way for many to play the game.

CHAPTER 2

CHI CHI

"The first time I played the Masters, I was so nervous I drank a bottle of rum before I teed off. I shot the happiest 83 of my life."

There is no more deserving golfer to follow Arnold Palmer than a man who has one of the most widely recognized names in golf: the world-famous and beloved Juan Antonio "Chi Chi" Rodriguez. Born in Puerto Rico in 1935, Chi Chi learned to play golf with clubs carved out of guava tree limbs and tin cans hammered into balls. He played on the PGA Tour from 1960 to 1981, winning eight events. Continuing his illustrious golfing career on the Senior (now Champions) Tour, Chi Chi confirmed his champion status, winning twenty-two tour titles. Rodriguez ranks sixth on the Champions Tour's all-time victory list and holds the tour record of having the most consecutive birdies (eight). His eight birdies not only secured his win at the 1987 Silver Page Classic, they gave him an unprecedented fourth straight victory in a single season. In 1992, the exclusive World Golf Hall of Fame inducted Chi Chi.

Chi Chi is famous for his prolific and impressive wins and for entertaining the galleries with his infamous birdie "toreador dance," born from an experience he had playing as a youth. Due to humble beginnings, he became a caddy at the age of six to help support the family. As his golf game improved, he began playing other caddies at the course, betting them five cents a hole. One day, after sinking a putt for a birdie, Chi Chi was all smiles, knowing he had just won five cents. Suddenly, his opponent advised him to put his hat over the hole quickly, as there was a toad in the cup. "If the toad jumps out of the hole and your ball pops out with the animal, the birdie doesn't count," the caddie said smugly.

From that moment on, Chi Chi started putting his hat over the hole whenever he made a birdie or eagle. When Chi Chi turned pro in 1960, he continued to do what became his signature hat act. He learned, however, that his frolicsome hat celebration was distracting some of the players, so he came up with another idea to dazzle the gallery—the toreador dance. Chi Chi pretended that the birdie was a "bull" and his putter was a "sword." Whenever he made a birdie, Chi Chi would take out his "sword" and stab the "bull." He then took a handkerchief out of his pocket and wiped the "blood" off his "sword."

This colorful golfer also had a humanitarian side. In 1979, he founded the Chi Chi Rodriguez Youth Foundation to help inner city kids make it in life. "If I made it, anybody can do it," said Chi Chi. "If I can help one kid become successful, that's all I ask for." As the recipient of countless honors, Chi Chi warmly received The Father of the Year Award in 1982. In 1990, he garnered the Caring for Kids Award. In 1991, he was given The Jackie Robinson Humanitarian Award, and in 1994, Chi Chi was inducted into the World Sports Humanitarian Hall of Fame, a most fitting tribute to one of the most popular golfers ever. Chi Chi Rodriguez ranks as highly as Arnold Palmer and Gary Player as one of golf's great goodwill ambassadors.

I first saw Chi Chi Rodriguez up close in 1997, at the Skins Game at the plush Rancho La Quinta Country Club in La Quinta, California. My wife Judy and I drove to the desert to soak up the perpetual sunshine and to watch the annual Skins Game at the new luxury country club. We arrived in time to witness a morning exhibition of trick and fancy shots performed by Chi Chi Rodriguez. I had seen him play in quite a few practice rounds, but didn't know he was a trick shot artist. The exhibition drew a large gallery to watch Chi Chi showcase his shot-making skills at Rancho La Quinta's driving range. The Puerto Rican golfer entertained the crowd for about thirty minutes with his bag of tricks. Among his repertoire of about twenty amazing shots, I vividly remember two that were astonishing and fun to watch.

On the first one, Chi Chi took out a 7-iron and hit the ball straight for the 165-yard carry to the practice green. The ball landed about ten feet from the flag. Everyone clapped for the great iron shot. His face relaxing into a broad grin, Chi Chi said, "Hey, folks, no need to clap. I'm a professional golfer, and I should be able to do that. Now, if I can pull off my next shot with the same iron, you can clap for me." With that, Chi Chi addressed the ball, then gripped the club, opened his stance, and hovered the leading edge (bottom) of the 7-iron to line up with the middle of the ball. He took a slow and carefully guided swing, struck the ball, and to everyone's amazement, the ball landed on the same green. With a big smile on his face, Chi Chi said, "Now, folks, you can clap for me!" He got a big round of applause from a delighted audience. How he turned his 7-iron into a magic wand is still a mystery to me.

For his grand finale trick shot, Chi Chi told the crowd, "I want you to carefully watch what I'm about to do, because I'm the only golfer in the world that can perform this famous trick." People perched on the edges of their seats, believing they were going to witness a Houdini-like, incredible feat. Chi Chi said, "I'm going to tee up two balls placed a foot apart. Using my driver, I'm going to hit the first ball and draw it out over the range, quickly step up to the second ball, hit it with a slice, and if all goes as intended, the two balls will cross over each other and collide in midair about 230 yards from here." I knew that Chi Chi was regarded as one of the game's finest shot-makers, able to work the ball left to right or right to left at will, but I thought to myself, *No way in hell can Chi Chi pull off this "out-of-the-world" trick shot.* Golf legend Lee Trevino might have believed the trick shot. In an interview with Guy Yocom of *Golf Digest,* Lee said, "Chi Chi Rodriguez had as good a pair of hands as anybody I ever saw, and more shots than you can imagine."

Chi Chi teed up the two balls and did exactly what he said he was going to do. He hit both balls in rapid succession. I could see the balls crossing in the air; they didn't hit in midair as he claimed. Chi Chi then commented, "Sorry, folks, give me one more try." He repeated the same steps, the balls crossing beautifully in the air and, from where I was seated, I truly thought for a few seconds that I was going to witness the greatest golf trick shot of all time. The two balls crossed over each other, but as before, they never collided. Chi Chi apologized, "I can't make 'em all of the time!" He tipped his straw hat, and in return received a well-deserved, standing ovation. To this day, I still wonder if Chi Chi ever pulled off his finale trick shot. It really doesn't matter. We were all entertained and spellbound by the act, and that's a trademark of a great trick artist and performer.

When I decided to add Chi Chi's autograph to my golf ball collection, my opportunity arose when the seniors returned to "Tuscany in California," Napa, for the fall Transamerica Championship at Silverado Country Club. I waited purposely for Chi Chi to finish up his round on the eighteenth green of the South Course. After putting out, Chi Chi began walking down the path toward the clubhouse, and autograph seekers, including myself, mobbed him. It was a very warm October day, and Chi Chi responded, "It's too hot here; let's go down to that large tree where there's shade." All autograph hounds quickly bolted for the tree, with me flying faster than a bullet to get there. Adept at muscling my way past kids, women, and men to get autographs, I was first in line to get Chi Chi's John Hancock.

As I handed Chi Chi my ball, he said, "Children first." Knowing how much Chi Chi loves kids, I wasn't surprised by this kind gesture. Three or four children came forward, and after Chi Chi signed the last item, I knew I was next because I made sure not to lose my place in line. As I handed Chi Chi the ball for the second time, he said, "Women next." I had no problem with the few women autograph seekers in the crowd going before me, as I was brought up to believe in the adage, "Ladies before gentlemen." After Chi Chi signed the last woman's hat, it came time for my sought-after Ch Chi Rodriguez autograph. As I handed the ball to Chi Chi for the third time to sign, he jokingly said, "Mexicans next." My eyeballs almost popped out from laughing so hard. Chi Chi also cracked up. I finally got my patiently awaited autograph from the crowd pleaser and one of the golf legends of all time, Chi Chi Rodriguez.

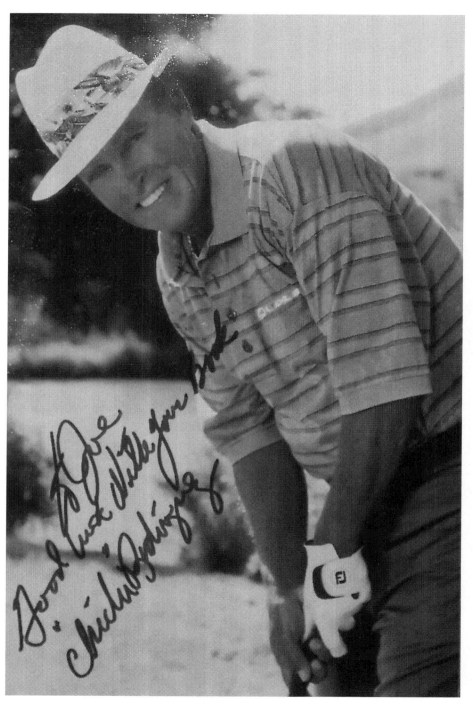

Gallery favorite, Chi Chi Rodriguez

CHAPTER 3

JACK LEMMON – A CUT ABOVE

"If you think it's hard to meet new people, try picking up the wrong ball."

For five years, I tried to obtain the legendary actor's autograph on a golf ball. I admired Lemmon's celebrity as a great actor, but I also enjoyed watching him pursue his golf hobby with amazing tenacity.

Jack Lemmon was born February 8, 1925, in Boston. In an acting career that spanned almost fifty years, Jack was nominated for best actor and best supporting actor awards for roles in eight movies, winning a best actor Oscar for the 1973 movie *Save the Tiger* and a best supporting actor Oscar for *Mister Roberts*, in 1955. He starred in such movies as *The Apartment* (1960), *The Odd Couple* (1960), *Days of Wine and Roses* (1962), and *Grumpy Old Men* (1993), to name just a few of the forty-seven movies in which he appeared.

The multitalented stage and television actor began playing in the AT&T Pebble Beach National Pro-Am in 1969, when the tournament was known as the Bing Crosby National Pro Amateur, or just the Crosby Clambake. The world's first celebrity golf tournament sparkled with PGA Tour professionals matched up with Hollywood stars and well-known sports figures. The celebrities came to measure their skills and delight the crowds with their on-course antics. Although Jack Lemmon was the perennial tournament favorite, his most famous achievement was not making the cut in thirty-four tries. His good friend and playing partner for eighteen years, PGA Tour professional Peter Jacobsen, told me, "We missed (making the cut) by one shot one time and missed by two shots twice." In 1998, Jack appeared to finally come close to making the cut, but El Nino spoiled his plans when heavy rains cancelled play. Even fate got into the act to stop Jack from playing on the weekend.

Everyone attending the AT&T Pebble Beach tournaments or watching Jack on television rooted for him to make the cut. If he could have made it through the third-round cut and played with the pros just once on a Sunday at Pebble Beach, the entire golf world would have celebrated. Once, Jack jokingly commented that he'd gladly trade one of his Oscars just to make the final round on the weekend.

I attended my first Pebble Beach AT&T Pro-Am in 1990 with Judy. In past years, Bing Crosby, Bob Hope, Phil Harris, Dean Martin, Tennessee Ernie Ford, Andy Williams, Jack Lemmon, and other colorful showbiz personalities delighted the crowd with their wit and great sense of humor. Tennessee Ford, telling of a golf experience at Pebble Beach, said, "Once I hit Dean Martin just as he was about to take a shot—knocked the bottle clean out of his hand."

I didn't realize that this Pro-Am is the only PGA tournament where amateurs play straight through to the final putt of the seventy-two-hole event, competing with their professional partners to make the cut. This Pro-Am also allowed eager galleries to click away on their cameras; otherwise, I wouldn't have been able to take the picture of Judy posing with legend Jack Nicklaus after he walked off Pebble Beach's eighteenth green. At the same time, I got Jack's signature (my second signed ball) on a Spyglass Hill logo ball for my collection.

Judy and Jack Nicklaus pause for a photo

In 1991, I returned to the AT&T Pebble Beach Pro-Am with a very good friend, Roger Dennis, and his son Danny. While driving to Pebble Beach, I told Roger that he would be meeting a friend of mine, one of the favorite celebrities entered in the event. (Truthfully, I had no celebrity lined up to meet Roger. I simply wanted to pull yet another prank on my friend.) Curious and eager to meet the mystery celebrity, Roger swallowed the bait—hook, line, and sinker.

When the three of us arrived, we began watching the pros and celebrities play at Poppy Hills. Eventually, we caught up with the popular U.S. Open champion, Payne Stewart, at the sixteenth hole and followed him in for the rest of his practice round. We then took the shuttle back to Pebble Beach to look for celebrities who might be on the practice putting green or hanging around the lodge. As we approached the green, I suddenly spied Jack Lemmon on the putting green. I also recognized his actor son, Chris, standing near him. Now was the perfect time to get my prankster pistons firing to pull off the practical joke on Roger by introducing him to the two-time Oscar-winning "mystery friend" of mine, Jack Lemmon. There was just one problem; I didn't know Jack Lemmon. So, how did I pull off the introduction?

Thanks to a call from Mother Nature, I got the lucky break I needed to solve my dilemma. I went into the lodge restroom and encountered Chris Lemmon. I decided to take a chance by asking Chris if he would ask his dad if my friend and I could have our picture taken with Jack. He said, "Sure, let's do it now!" The two of us walked out to the practice green, and while Chris went to get his dad, I quickly told Roger that he was now going to meet my friend, Jack Lemmon, the best loved actor in Hollywood. I'm sure Roger didn't believe me, but when he saw Jack Lemmon walking toward us, his expression turned wide eyed and star struck. Roger fell for my story. Chris brought Jack over, we introduced ourselves, and Danny took the picture with his camera. Thanks to my stroke of luck meeting Chris in the men's room, my practical joke on Roger worked, at least for a brief moment, before I introduced myself to Jack. As it turned out, the prank I played on Roger backfired on me.

Spectators around the green that afternoon must have wondered why two guys had their picture taken with Jack Lemmon. I could have told the crowd that Jack and I started in vaudeville together in Pittsburgh in the

1930s. Check out Roger's humorously written article, "Old Timer's Reunion," taken from Allstate's regional employee publication, *Golden Gate UPDATE*, April 1991.

"Old Timer's Reunion"

by Roger Dennis
Sales Territory V

The Pebble Beach AT&T Pro Am Golf Tournament held on January 31 through February 3, on the Monterey Peninsula, brought about an interesting reunion. It all started when Market Sales Manager Joe Galiardi called me a few weeks before the tournament to ask if I was planning to join the spectators during the four days of play.

Not having been to the Pro-Am for several years, I quickly said I was ready to go, and we set the date for the first practice round on January 30. For the week or so leading up to the tournament, Joe kept telling me I was in for a "special treat." He'd get all excited about it but wouldn't tell me what it was, which really aroused my curiosity.

Joe picked me up at 6:30 a.m., and we headed for Pebble Beach. He was so excited he couldn't stop talking. Now, I know Joe enjoys his golf, but his anticipation was so great that I was afraid the excitement was going to kill him! All of this over seeing a few golfers?

We spent the day at Poppy Hills Golf Course following the foursome of celebrities and professional golfers. Joe came well prepared for the day and knew exactly who was playing with whom, at what course, and at which hole. I was beginning to think that age was catching up with him, but his eyes still looked so clear that I gave him the benefit of the doubt.

Joe was euphoric as he obtained an autographed ball from one of the top pros, Payne Stewart, to add to his collection of Nicklaus and Palmer! Later, he even persuaded one of the Gatlin Brothers to sign a special Grand Old Opry golf ball for him. I thought all of this was the big surprise he talked about for weeks, but just then he said, "Are you ready for the big surprise?"

At that, Joe had me follow him over to the practice putting green at the famed Pebble Beach Lodge. Out on the putting green were many of the celebrities and pros who had finished their day's play and were sharpening their skills. Jack Lemmon was the best known and most popular celebrity there, and as such, everyone wanted his picture or autograph. Jack was ignoring them all, as he seriously wanted to do well in this tournament.

Jack was oblivious to the crowd until Joe started singing, "I'm A Yankee Doodle Dandy" loud enough for Jack and everyone else to hear. Jack turned around, saw Joe, and came running to greet him. They embraced, did a few high fives, and then finished the song together including a little dance step number that was perfectly executed.

Now came the BIG SURPRISE! Joe introduced me to Jack Lemmon and started to explain how he and Jack started in vaudeville together in Pittsburgh, PA in the 1930s. Their act was called "Jack and Jill," but that's another story!

So that brings us to the explanation of this picture of Jack Lemmon, Joe Galiardi, and myself. That's the story, but there is one last moral to this story. There's no fool like an April fool! Sorry, Joe, the devil made me do it!

Joe, Jack, and Roger

More than fifteen hundred employees read this hilarious article. I can't count the number of fellow workers who read the story and truly believed it, even though the publication was distributed on April Fool's Day. Employees approached me later and commented, "Oh, Joe, I didn't know that you and Jack Lemmon started in vaudeville in Pittsburgh in the 1930s!" "Joe, are you that old?" "Joe, I didn't know you could sing and dance." After the article came out, I finally realized I had met my match with Roger and haven't pulled a practical joke on him since.

After we had our pictures taken with Jack Lemmon, my first thought was how stupid of me to have brought only two golf balls to the tournament to be signed. Payne Stewart autographed one of the balls at the eighteenth green at Poppy Hills earlier in the day. Country singer Sam Gatlin of the Gatlin Brothers signed the second ball, a logo ball from Grand Old Opry House in Nashville. I thought I blew my chances to get Jack's signature. However, it didn't take long for me to realize that even if I did have an extra ball in my pocket, I probably wouldn't have gotten Jack's autograph. There were many autograph hounds surrounding the green, asking Jack to sign various items, but he ignored them all, as he took his putting practice very seriously in preparation for the start of the tournament the next day.

In 1992, I attended another AT&T Pebble Beach Pro-Am practice round and found Jack Lemmon practicing his putting before teeing off. As Jack walked off the green, several dozen onlookers asked Jack to sign various items, me among them. Jack said, "Sorry folks, I need to get to the first tee; catch me later." I didn't see him for the remainder of the day. I thought, *Oh, well, I'll get his autograph next year.*

After my first year in 1990, I went to the Pro-Am every year, but only for one day and always on the Wednesday practice-round day when all pros and celebrities would be present. I always brought a few balls to be signed and came home every year with some signatures to add to my collection. Jack Lemmon's signature was not among them. I always asked Jack for his autograph. He always responded, "Catch me later." For four years, I didn't get discouraged, because I was acquiring many great autographs from pros and celebrities at the AT&T Pro Am tournaments. I also learned that if one wants to be a serious autograph seeker, one must possess two virtues: patience and perseverance. Fortunately, I was blessed with both.

In 1996, due to unplayable wet conditions at Pebble Beach Golf Links, the AT&T Celebrity Shootout was held at the Peter Hayes nine-hole executive par-3 golf course, located across the street from Pebble Beach. The shootout is an exhibition that brings out golf and movie fans alike, eager to see up close some of their favorite stars hack around the course. Jack Lemmon was one of the show biz stars in the shootout that year, bravely putting his game on display. I didn't watch the popular event, but I was there at the finish to try again for the umpteenth time to get Jack's signature on a golf ball. As Jack walked off the course, at least twenty fans waited to get his John Hancock. As he had done many times before, he told the crowd, "Sorry folks, I have to run; catch me later." A voice inside my head whispered, *Don't give up.*

After the crowd dispersed, I followed Jack down the dirt path toward the lodge. He wasn't aware that I was following him. I found him sitting on the back bumper of his car, changing into his street shoes. I asked, "Jack, will you be kind enough to sign this golf ball?" If he responded, "Catch me later," I planned say something pithy and wise, a real comeback, something to feel proud of. I just had no idea what that would be. I felt utter shock when he graciously signed it without a word. I gasped in surprise, happily thanked him, and walked away triumphantly with my prize possession, a Jack Lemmon autographed golf ball. I felt like a giddy six-year-old kid who had just gotten a new puppy.

I prominently display Jack Lemmon's autographed golf ball in my golf room along with the other 220 signed balls. His ball stands as a testament to the patience and determination it sometimes takes to get a celebrity's autograph. Jack said good-bye to the world in 2001, and the AT&T Pebble Beach National Pro Am will never be the same without him.

CHAPTER 4

THE BETTY HICKS STORY

"See it, feel it, hit it."

How many women or men do you know who excelled in the following categories: professional golfer, college golf coach, journalist, photographer, pilot, gourmet cook, historian, author, lecturer, and actor? I know only one person who claims to have worn all these hats: Elizabeth "Betty" Hicks. Women's golf has come a long way thanks to this talented and incredible woman, whose professional victory at the 1944 All-American Open sowed the seeds for the establishment of the Ladies Professional Golf Association (LPGA) in 1950.

I first heard the name Betty Hicks in 1983, shortly after I married Judy, who lived in a Spanish-designed condominium development in Cupertino, California, called Casa de Anza. I moved into Judy's condo upon returning from our honeymoon in Hawaii. At the time, we were avid tennis players and were fortunate to live within a racket toss from the tennis facility. While playing tennis, Judy and I observed a woman who appeared to be in her fifties walking her dog around the complex. We learned that her name was Betty Hicks and that she was a golfer of some notoriety.

In 1986, we moved to Rancho Deep Cliff in Cupertino. Twenty years later, while selecting the contents of my book, I remembered Betty Hicks and wondered if I should research her career in golf to earn a spot in my book. If she was, in fact, a true pioneer, I wanted to get her autograph on a golf ball and interview her.

At the early stages of writing my book, I wasn't sure if Betty was still alive. I followed advice about checking on original addresses, so I traveled five minutes to our old homestead to learn if Betty still lived at Casa de Anza. I strolled up to the address I remembered and rang the doorbell. Betty's caretaker, Elizabeth Hunter, answered the door and explained that Betty indeed still lived there. She confirmed the fact that Betty was a pioneer in women's golf. Elizabeth explained that Betty was very instrumental in the establishment of the Women's Professional Golf Association, the forerunner to today's LPGA. I thanked her and headed back home, delighted to know I had tracked Betty to her address. A week later, I called her and explained who I was and mentioned our living at Casa de Anza in the early 1980s, although I couldn't be sure that Betty remembered us. I explained that I wanted to interview her for my book and asked if I could stop by and see her. Her response: "I'm not sure it's a good idea for you to come by because my dog bites." I said, "Betty, don't worry about that. I have a theory about dogs. I believe they can sense if a person likes them or not. I like dogs and dogs like me. So please, don't worry about your dog biting me." With the reassurance on my part, Betty agreed to see me, and I quickly jumped into the car, driving the short distance in record time. When I arrived at Betty's condo, I rang the doorbell. After waiting what seemed like an eternity, the front door slowly opened and just as it did, a tiny Yorkshire terrier exploded out, went immediately for my ankle, and the little turd nipped me.

There goes my theory about dog biting.

Inside the condo, I heard a woman's voice say, "Chip, stop that!" But Chip, the gallant protector, wouldn't let me move one inch toward his mistress. Chip kept growling at me and made threatening moves to bite me again, so I froze and maintained the "Statue of Liberty" position until Betty finally was able to corner Chip and put him on his leash. A cute story, but it doesn't end there. It wasn't easy walking into Betty's condo with Chip still trying to take a small chunk from my ankle, but I finally made it to the living room, eager to sit down on the sofa to get the full story.

Betty's living room resembled my golf room, completely filled with her private collection of wonderful memorabilia from yesteryear. The first item catching my eye was the beautiful portrait hanging over the fireplace of Betty in golf attire. I then recognized on the wall a charcoal drawing of the late Harvey Penick, whose *Little Red Book* became the largest-selling sports book in history. At last count, the runaway *New York Times* bestseller had been published in seventeen languages. The third item drawing my attention was a yellow eighteenth-hole golf flag from Brookline Country Club, where twenty-one-year-old Betty Hicks won the 1941 Women's U.S. Amateur Championship.

I noticed many other charcoal drawings on the living room walls of famous golfers, both male and female, with whom Betty had played with in her early years. Much to my surprise, a closer look revealed that her signature appeared on all of the drawings. Two drawings particularly caught my attention. One was the legendary Hollywood actress Katharine Hepburn, and the other was world-heavyweight boxing champion Joe Louis. I made a mental note to ask Betty why these two unlikely sketches would appear in her collection of golf memorabilia.

However, before I could chat with Betty, it was clear that I would still have to romance Chip, who didn't take kindly to my presence. He never took his eyes off me and was ready to resume his ankle attacks if I made the slightest move. The first words from Betty's mouth, in a near shout over the yapping, "Chip is my protector." For the first five minutes, Chip didn't stop growling and barking. Eventually, he simmered down. At one point, he jumped up beside me on the couch and warily allowed me to pat his head for a brief moment. Still, he gave me the old "stink-eye" for the rest of the visit.

I turned on my tape recorder and suggested that we begin by talking about her extraordinary life and golf career.

Betty, how did you get started in golf?

"I took a golf class when I was a freshman at Long Beach City College (1937). I immediately got hooked on the sport and became more interested in golf than on my studies. Observing my interest in the game, my father, a high school principal, gave me the option of taking my college money to pursue a career in golf or use the money to complete my college education. I took the money and started on my career in golf."

(Before golf, Betty's first athletic interest was softball. In her book, *My Life: From Fairway to Airway,* she wrote, "As a pitcher on the college softball team, I could throw a wicked curve of blinding velocity and a baffling change up. In one afternoon in 1937, I pitched two no-hit games, one against Pomona CC and one against Glendale CC.")

What happened after you decided to make a career out of golf?

"I started taking golf lessons, practicing constantly, and entering tournaments in Southern California. In 1938, I won the Long Beach City Championship, but my big breakthrough came in 1939 when I got to the semifinal round in both the U.S. Women's Amateur and the Western Amateur championships. Encouraged by my high finish in these two national events, I intensified my practice regime by hitting five hundred shots daily on the range and playing a round of golf each day. I also practiced hitting sand shots out of the soft sandy beach at Long Beach."

Wow! When did you have time to do anything else?

"I didn't. Only after completing my daily rigorous practice schedule could I go home."

So, when and where did you win your first big golf tournament?

"In 1940, I won the South Atlantic Championship and the Titleholder Championship (now classified by the LPGA as a major championship). The year 1940 turned out to be a banner year for me. On the Florida swing, I won three tournaments and was the medalist winner in the Women's Western Golf Association Derby. To tell the truth, the tournament I was most proud of winning was the 1941 U.S. Women's Amateur Championship at the Brookline Country Club in Massachusetts, at age twenty-one. Shortly after my national victory, I turned professional."

(Women were not allowed in clubhouse in 1941. Betty received her Robert Cox trophy on the porch at The Brookline Country Club.)

Were you one of the first women professionals in the country?

"No. I believe I was among the first fifteen women in the United States to turn pro. Helen Hicks (no relation) from New York was the first female pro golfer. She turned pro after winning the U.S. Women's Amateur Championship in the early 1930s."

In doing my homework for this interview, I found out that you were named Female Athlete of the Year by the Associated Press, in 1941. (Her counterpart that year was New York Yankee Joe DiMaggio, Male Athlete of the Year.) **What an honor to achieve at such an early age. You**

must have been thrilled upon learning that you were AP's choice for the Female Athlete award.

"I was. It definitely came as a surprise. But my win at Brookline still stands out as my most memorable victory."

OK, now tell me what happened after you turned pro in 1941?

"Not much happened. In those days, there wasn't a women's professional golf tour, and there weren't many women's golf tournaments. You have to remember that the game of golf historically had been a wealthy man's leisure pastime. We had to overcome the social barriers. The few women professionals like me had to make a living by giving private lessons and putting on golf clinics. Shortly after World War II began, I joined the U.S. Coast Guard."

So, no golf for you during the war years?

"Oh, yes! I wanted to serve my country in the war, but the Coast Guard released me from active duty and put me in the reserve so that I could play golf exhibitions with movie stars and other celebrities to raise money for the Red Cross and the War Bond Campaign. I was also a recruiter for the Coast Guard during the war."

Who were some of your favorite celebrities you played with during the war years?

"My two favorites were Bing Crosby and Bob Hope. I even played an exhibition match with Joe Louis, who was the heavyweight boxing champion of the world at that time. He was an avid golfer."

Tell me about the match with Joe Louis.

"Well, the match took place in Detroit, Joe's hometown. I knew that Joe Louis was reputed to be a big gambler and a very good golfer. I think his handicap was a six or seven. Just before we teed off, Joe asked me, "Betty, how much are we going to play for today?" Not being a gambler, I said, "How about an ice cream cone?" I could tell from the expression on his face that the champ wanted to play for bigger stakes, but he agreed to the bet. He was a perfect gentleman that day."

Who won?

"Mr. Louis treated."

Any favorite tales playing with Bob Hope and Bing Crosby?

"I played many exhibitions with them. They were crowd-pleasers and fun to be around. Bob Hope was a kick. Every so often, he would hum a tune as he teed it up. After hitting a great shot or making a spectacular putt, Bob would occasionally make everyone double up with laughter by doing his famous vaudeville soft-shoe routine. It was delightful theater. Here's a funny story about Bob Hope. One time, Bob's caddie said to him, 'Mr. Hope, watch the greens today; they've been mowed this morning.' Bob replied, 'What time?' On the wall behind you is a framed scorecard showing that I played an exhibition match with Bing Crosby, Bob Hope, and Carol Friese at the Topeka Country Club in Kansas. Carol was a fine amateur from Portland, Oregon. On the scorecard, it shows we played the first twelve holes and seventeen and eighteen. We knew we weren't going to be able to finish the match because of darkness, so we decided to skip holes thirteen through sixteen in order to complete the match and not disappoint the gallery."

All three of Betty's partners signed the unique scorecard. Betty shot a 39 on the front nine; Bing Crosby, 40; Bob Hope, 42; and Carol Friese, 41.

Betty, I notice on the wall a sketch you did of Katharine Hepburn. What prompted you to do a charcoal drawing of her?

"I had a cameo role with her and Spencer Tracy in a film called *Pat and Mike*. The 1951 movie was about a star woman athlete played by Katharine Hepburn and was filmed around Los Angeles, with many golf scenes taking place at the Riviera Country Club. A few years after they made the movie, I decided to do a charcoal sketch of Kate and have her autograph it. I mailed the portrait to her, but she returned it unsigned along with a signed letter explaining why she didn't sign the drawing. I framed her reply with the sketch."

Katharine Houghton Hepburn

11 – 6 – 1990

Dear Betty Hicks,

I'm sorry but I do not sign photographs for people unless I really know them—even a photograph of a sketch of a photograph. So here it is again—to be frank—I think your sketch is better than the photograph—good for you.

K. Hepburn (signed)

Betty, you had to be very disappointed when you received Katharine Hepburn's letter.

"I was. I can't say that we were really good friends, but I did meet Kate on the set, and we saw each other quite often while the scenes were being shot on the golf course."

Betty (left) walking with Katharine Hepburn during filming of *Pat and Mike*

Were you in any other movies?

"Yes, I was in *The Life of Riley* (1949) with William Bendix. The film was based on the radio program, *The Life of Riley*, a very popular radio comedy series of the 1940s." (William Bendix was an Academy Award-nominated American film actor. One of his well-known movie roles was portraying legendary baseball home run king, Babe Ruth, in *The Babe Ruth Story (1948)*. Ironically, William Bendix played the part of Babe in the movie, because as a youngster he was a batboy for the New York Yankees and watched baseball's first great slugger hit some of his lifetime total of 714 home runs.)

William Bendix getting a chipping lesson from Betty

Betty, let's get back to golf. You told me that you played a lot of exhibitions during the war. Were there any professional tournaments being played during the war years?

"Yes. I won the 1943 All-American Open (a golf tournament on the PGA Tour) at the Tam O'Shanter Country Club in Illinois and won the same tournament again in 1944. The tournament featured two open events, one for men and one for women. I earned five hundred dollars for my win in 1944. Byron Nelson won the men's title that year and pocketed twenty-seven thousand dollars. I wasn't very happy with the small amount of money I won compared to Byron's winnings. Actually, the prize money disparity turned out to be a blessing. Shortly after the tournament, our small group of professional women (three) got together and decided it was time to start our own association and establish a women's professional tour."

What happened?

"We formed the Women's Professional Golf Association in 1944, and I became the first president of the WPGA. We struggled in the early years and had to give exhibitions and clinics to make a living. I was fortunate to gain sponsorship from Wilson Sporting Goods Company. I did a lot of travelling in those days, working tirelessly for more opportunity and equal prize money for female golfers in the early beginnings of our association. It wasn't easy getting our tour started, but we overcame the odds and we paved the way for what became the Ladies Professional Golf Association in 1950. I'm proud to have been one of the early pioneers of women's professional golf."

According to the book, *Golf Legends of All Time,* "In the late 1940s, Babe Zaharias, Patty Berg, and Betty Hicks reformed the Women's Professional Golf Association into the Ladies PGA, and they began developing its tour."

Betty, why the name change from Women's to Ladies in 1950?

"Babe Zaharias' manager, Fred Corcoran, was responsible for making the name change. He felt that the word 'ladies' sounded better than 'women's.'"

Are there any other tournaments you played in worth mentioning in my book?

"I was a runner-up twice in the U.S. Women's Open in 1948 and 1954, losing both times to Babe Zaharias. (In 1950, the Associated Press voted Babe Woman Athlete of the Half-Century.) I ended up winning eleven pro events."

Betty, I'm sure you would have won many more pro events had you not been tied down to your sponsor and other organizational commitments.

"Probably. I did put on many golf clinics for the Wilson Sporting Goods Company, the National Golf Foundation, and the LPGA National Golf School. I figure I made some fifteen hundred appearances during my long career."

At a second interview with Betty and her tiny but gallant protector, in April 2007, I learned that Chip encountered the wrath of a Santa Clara County animal officer after the Yorkie bit a delivery person on the ankle. As Betty stated in her book about the occurrence, "Chip and I had a serious discussion about the incident, but he did not learn from his quarantine."

I read that you wrote two books and co-authored two others plus hundreds of articles for such magazines as *Saturday Evening Post, Look, Golf Digest, Sports Illustrated,* and *Golf for Women.* I also learned that you earned your BA with a double major in aeronautics and journalism from San Jose State University in 1974.

"That's right. It only took me thirty-seven years and eight different schools from the time I started college to get my degree."

I know you coached San Jose State's women's golf team in the mid 1970s. How many years did you coach there?

"Two years." (Betty was inducted into the San Jose Sports Hall of Fame in 2002.)

Why a degree in aeronautics?

"As a young girl, I became interested in aviation by seeing Amelia Earhart (the first woman to pilot a plane across the Atlantic Ocean) fly from our local Long Beach airfield. During the 1950s, in addition to competing on tour, I was the LPGA's publicity director and traveled thirty-five thousand to forty thousand miles a year in my car. I finally decided that I had enough of the woes of driving and enrolled in a flight school in Los Coyotes in Southern California. In 1957, I bought my first airplane, a Cessna 172. I calculated that I saved one whole year of time by flying instead of driving to all of my destinations." (In 2001, Betty was inducted into the International Forest of Friendship, an aviation hall of fame, in Atchison, Kansas, Amelia Earhart's birthplace, for her many major contributions to aviation.)

Betty boarding her plane with golf bag

You did lots of writing for Ernest Jones, one of the great golf teachers of the twenty-first century, and for Harvey Penick. I must ask you about Penick's comment in his *Little Red Book*. In the chapter, "Some of the Women in My Life," here is what he wrote about you.

Betty had a long, loose swing and tended to lose control at the top of her backswing. When this happened, she hit a bad hook. I told her in all good humor that she swung the club like an old cow's tail. I didn't mean to hurt her feelings, but she told me (joking, I hope) she would never forgive me.

Betty, were you joking when you told Mr. Penick you would never forgive him for his cruel remark about your swing?

"Of course I was. I knew he was just kidding me. I wrote articles for Harvey for over twenty years. We were best of friends. He was a great teacher."

Now, for the $64,000 question. Who was the best female and male golfer you ever saw?

"Mickey Wright and Ben Hogan. Mickey had the best swing in all of golf. It was poetry in motion. Harvey Penick always said that Mickey was the greatest woman player of all time."

Mickey Wright ranks second in all-time LPGA victories with eighty-two, behind Kathy Whitworth's eighty-eight wins. After reading Betty's and Harvey's comments about Mickey Wright, I knew I had to have her autograph in my ball collection. Luckily for me, Betty gave me Mickey's address in Florida. I wrote to Mickey and explained about the book I was writing and the chapter devoted to her good friend, Betty Hicks. I also sent a golf ball to be autographed. Within two weeks, I joyfully received the ball with Mickey's beautifully hand-written signature on it, along with the following note.

Joe,

Betty Hicks has so many wonderful attributes. It's hard to know where to start. Back in 1955 when I joined the tour, she and Betsy Rawls made me feel welcome. Betty had a simple, sound golf swing. She, of course, is a wonderful writer, pilot, and teacher. Thanks to her, the LPGA is what it is today.

And Ben Hogan?

"He was certainly one of golf's all-time great champions. We played a friendly match at his home course, Colonial Country Club in Ft. Worth, Texas, to raise money for the War Relief Fund. He was a very nice person. No one was a better golfer than Ben Hogan at that time."

Betty, how many holes in one have you had?

"Five."

I mentioned to you on the phone that I was the high bidder on eBay for a manual you wrote called *SIMPLICITY!* that described the Ernest Jones method of teaching golf. What advice did this famous instructor give you one week before you entered the 1941 U.S. Women's Amateur Championship?

"I was an intense student of the Ernest Jones theory of swinging the golf club. I was having tempo problems with my swing when I went to see him for help. After watching me hit a few balls, Ernest showed a glimpse of his talent by bringing out an old Victrola phonograph, hand-cranked it and played a 78 record, "The Blue Danube Waltz." He told me to swing to the music and before I knew it, my tempo was back. I won the Amateur the next week, swinging to the Strauss waltz embedded in my mind."

What other books did you write?

I wrote a book on gourmet cooking, *Travels with a Golf Tour Gourmet.* I also co-authored *Patty Sheehan on Golf.* Patty had a beautiful and natural swing. Her game was always so consistent. She had so many satisfying wins on the LPGA Tour." (I mailed a letter to Patty Sheehan requesting her autograph on a golf ball. I also told her about the book I was writing and the chapter I had written about her close friend Betty Hicks. The Hall of Famer signed the ball and enclosed this short letter.)

Joe,

I've always been a Betty Hicks fan, ever since she saw in me what perhaps others didn't. She saw my "BD" (Burning Desire). She believed in me and took care of my golfing needs more than once. She's so knowledgeable about the game of golf. I also admire her brains and tenacity in learning and teaching flying. I will always admire her for her many contributions to golf, flying, writing, and photography. She is one great lady.

Have you written other books?

"I wrote one other with Ellen Griffin, a *Golf Manual for Teachers*, in 1949."

(In 1989, the LPGA established the annual Ellen Griffin Rolex Award honoring the female or male golf teacher who made a major contribution to the teaching of golf. Betty Hicks was the recipient of this prestigious award in 1999 for her important role in the establishment of the LPGA and in teaching the game of golf to women.)

Betty, what was the best part of your game?

"Sand bunker shots. I was taught by one of the best at getting out of sand traps, John Revolta. I took lessons from him at the Evanston Golf Club in Illinois. John played on the PGA Tour in the 1930s and '40s. He won quite a few PGA tournaments, including a PGA championship."

Finally, I'm going to ask you a question that has been asked of Jack Nicklaus and many other great golfers. If you had one last round of golf to play, which course would you choose to play?

"Riviera Country Club."

(Rated among the very finest golf courses, Riviera is located in Pacific Palisades, inside the city limits of Los Angeles. Betty was a teaching pro at various country clubs in Southern California, including the well-known Riviera CC.)

Betty, I can't thank you enough for giving me the time to chat with you about your life and the early growth and development of women's professional golf. You've had an exciting and incredible career in golf. As a small way of thanking you, I would like to take you to lunch at your favorite restaurant. Where would you like to go?

"The Blue Pheasant." (A long-established restaurant in Cupertino.)

Betty and I had lunch at the Blue Pheasant on VE (Victory in Europe) Day, May 8, 2007. I too scored a victory in being fortunate to have had the wonderful opportunity to interview one of the true pioneers of women's golf, a great woman, and a newfound friend. Considering how hard she campaigned for better prize money and equality for today's professional women golfers, Betty Hicks is indeed the Billie Jean King of golf.

Betty was inducted into the LPGA T & CP (Teaching and Club Professional) Hall of Fame in 2000 (inaugural class) along with legendary LPGA pros

Patty Berg, Louise Suggs, and Peggy Kirk Bell. Betty also was inducted into the International Women's Sports Hall of Fame, the California Golf Writers Hall of Fame, and the California Golf Hall of Fame, making her a member of six halls of fame.

Betty's autobiography, *My Life: From Fairway to Airway*, published in 2006, gives a fresh perspective on the beginnings of women's professional golf.

CHAPTER 5

THE MERRY MEX

*"When it comes to the game of life, I figure
I've played the whole course."*

Born in Texas in a small four-room wooden house with no electricity or plumbing, Lee Trevino rose from poverty to become one of the best ball-strikers in the game. Remarkably, he taught himself how to play golf by trial and error. Not known for having a classic swing, Trevino once said, "The only thing that matters in golf is the score you put on the board." The man, known as the Merry Mex, did post some great scores during his career, winning 29 PGA Tour tournaments including six majors, two apiece in the British, U.S. Open and PGA Championships. Joining the Senior Tour (now the Champions Tour) in 1990, Lee went on a victorious rampage, winning twenty-four events in the first five years. He ended up winning twenty-nine Champions Tour victories, following Hale Irwin on the all-time Champions Tour win list. Lee can boost of winning eighty-four tournaments in his epic career. Lee played for the United States in six Ryder Cups and came away with an impressive record of 17-7-6 win-loss-half record. He was captain of the Ryder Cup in 1985. The Mexican-American icon won the Hickok Belt as the top professional athlete of 1971. He was inducted into the World Golf Hall of Fame in 1981.

Trevino was very lucky to survive a freak lightning strike in 1975 while playing in the Western Open in Chicago. Although he sustained permanent damage to his back, he still could joke about it with this famous quote,

"If you are caught on a golf course during a storm and afraid of lightning, hold up a 1-iron. Not even God can hit a 1-iron."

Known for his wit, Lee commented about the fifty-and-over tour, saying, "One of the nice things about the Senior Tour is that we can take a cart and cooler. If your game is not going well, you can always have a picnic."

In 1995, I found Trevino where I obtained many other autographs from the senior players, at the Silverado Country Club. Lee, a gallery favorite at the Transamerica Senior Golf Championship, had finished the eighteenth hole on the South Course and was besieged by a crowd of jostling autograph hounds as he hurriedly walked off the green. Without stopping to sign autographs, Lee told everyone that he had to report immediately to the resort's conference center for a post-press interview. All fans respected his wishes, except me. Determined to get his autograph, I followed Trevino down the path that led to the conference center, hoping to get the golf legend's signature after the interview ended. As Lee met the reporter at the center's front entrance, I positioned myself behind a large white pillar about fifteen feet away to listen in on the interview. I must have been quite conspicuous to Lee and the reporter, but neither said a word about my presence. I felt uncomfortable standing so close to them, but I was there on a mission. I had to have an autograph from one of the most popular golfers the game has ever seen.

The interview lasted for about ten minutes, and when I heard the reporter ask his last question, I nearly swallowed my tongue. "Lee, why don't you like to give autographs?" *Oh, no!* I thought, *Now what am I going to do?* If I had known that Lee didn't like to give fans some ink, I wouldn't have put myself in this predicament. My initial reaction was to quietly slip away, but my fearless side told me to stay and grab the chance for that special sought-after signed ball. "It's not that I don't like to give autographs. The problem is so many of my shirts get ruined by spectators sticking me with ink pens while they're shoving all kinds of items in my face to get signed," Lee answered. "I can almost count on losing a couple of shirts a week because of ink marks."

As Lee turned away from the reporter to walk back toward the players' locker room, I made the decision to go for it. With golf ball and pen in hand, I stepped out from behind the pillar and bravely asked him for his autograph, expecting the worst. I truly was sweating this one out! However, the anxiety I experienced was all for naught.

Trevino, a real gentleman, took my Sharpie and signed the ball without saying a word. I thanked him and walked away on cloud nine. Elated and proud of myself for having the fortitude to approach Lee for his autograph, I began to feel like I had what it took to assemble one of the largest private autographed golf ball collections in the United States.

CHAPTER 6

FRANK SINATRA CELEBRITY GOLF INVITATIONAL

"May you live to be 100 and may the last voice you hear be mine."
Frank Sinatra

In February of 2001, while vacationing in La Quinta, California, about thirty-five miles east of Palm Springs, I read in the local newspaper that the Frank Sinatra Celebrity Golf Tournament would begin the following day at the Desert Willow Golf Resort in Palm Desert. The article didn't list the names of the celebrities playing in the charity event, founded by singer and actor Frank Sinatra in 1988 to raise funds for the Barbara Sinatra Children's Center. The paper mentioned that one of the greatest male movie actors of all time, Gregory Peck, was co-host of the Sinatra Tournament. I thought to myself, *I'd be happy to just have a mere glimpse of this Academy Award winner, much less have him sign a golf ball for my collection.*

I decided to go to the opening day of the popular tournament to collect autographs, not knowing which celebrities would show up with their new swings or new sets of clubs. I had a hunch the day would bring some real surprises. I took a small, black leather case containing eight brand-new golf balls, hoping I could get them autographed that morning. I was counting on some of the celebrities arriving early to the course to warm up before the event started.

Johnny Lujack

"You just don't feel good with a tie."

As I walked down the path leading to the driving range, I was startled to see the name "Johnny Lujack" on one of the golf carts parked near the range. There he was, our little town's famous hero and one of my boyhood idols, sitting in the cart alone.

Although we came from the same hometown of Connellsville, Pennsylvania, I had never met the great Notre Dame quarterback Johnny Lujack. I had certainly heard all about him when he was quarterbacking the powerhouse Notre Dame team in the years following World War II. Johnny left ND in his sophomore year to serve nearly three years in the U.S. Navy, returning in time for the 1946 season. I saw him in action in 1947 when the undefeated Notre Dame team came to Pittsburgh and blew out Pitt 40 to 6.

I walked over to Johnny, introduced myself, and told him I grew up in Connellsville. We had a very pleasant conversation. I couldn't believe my good fortune to meet and talk with one of the best college football quarterbacks of all time. In addition to his two-time All-American status, Johnny led Notre Dame to three National Championships, won the Heisman Trophy in 1947, and was voted Associated Press Male Athlete of the Year in 1947, beating out New York's Joe DiMaggio.

Playing during an era of two-way players, Johnny also played defensive back for the Fighting Irish. He made the most famous tackle in Notre Dame history. In 1946, in New York's Yankee Stadium, first-ranked Army played second-ranked Notre Dame. In a scoreless tie and only minutes remaining in the game, Johnny made a game-saving, open-field tackle of All-American Doc Blanchard (Heisman Trophy winner in 1945), at the eleven-yard line, cutting off a certain Army touchdown in an historic game that ended 0-0. If it weren't for Johnny's famed tackle, Notre Dame would not have gone undefeated in 1946. Both teams remained undefeated for the rest of the season, but Notre Dame finished first in AP rankings. The 1946 matchup of Army and Notre Dame was considered one of the best football games of the century.

Johnny was still a handsome man at age seventy-six. He carried a single-digit golf handicap, and even the U.S. Postal Service knew his hometown.

When my sister graduated from Penn State, she went to work for a company in Cincinnati. A few years later, a fellow Penn Stater wanted to get in touch with her but didn't have Rose's address. However, she did remember that my sister grew up in Johnny Lujack's hometown. She addressed the envelope to Rose M. Galiardi, c/o Johnny Lujack's hometown, Pennsylvania. The letter was delivered to my parents' home in Connellsville. I jokingly told Johnny the letter would have arrived there even if the woman had addressed the envelope to Johnny Lujack's hometown, U.S.A. He had a good laugh.

Getting Johnny Lujack's prized autograph was a great start and gave me an inkling that today was going to be "my day" for getting sought-after signatures from stars of stage, screen, and the sports arena.

One down, seven to go!

Ralph Kiner

"You know what they say about Chicago. If you don't like the weather, wait fifteen minutes."

While talking with Johnny Lujack, I noticed the name of another boyhood idol of mine, Ralph Kiner. The last time I saw Ralph Kiner was in 1953 in a Pittsburgh Pirates baseball uniform. Ralph was alone. I walked over to his cart, introduced myself and began the conversation by telling him I grew up in the Pittsburgh area and watched him blast many of his home runs at classic Forbes Field. I was star struck, talking to the greatest home run slugger of my youth.

Ralph Kiner put on a Pittsburgh Pirates uniform in 1946, at age twenty-three, and led the National League that year with twenty-three home runs. In his first seven years with the Pirates, he led the National League in home runs. No baseball player has matched that record since. Today, he still holds the Major League record for hitting eight home runs in four consecutive days, set in 1947, the year he hit fifty-one four-baggers. The power slugger had his best season in 1949, when he led the league in home runs with fifty-four and batted .310. He was elected to the Hall of Fame in 1975. Ralph Kiner was the first National League player to ask for and receive a salary of $100,000 for a season.

Ralph Kiner looked impressive for his age at seventy-eight. He seemed pleased with my knowledge of his baseball stats and playing days in "The Steel City." I had no problem getting his desirable autograph. I thanked him and went merrily looking for more celebrities.

Two down, six more to go.

Jason Giambi

"That stuff didn't help me hit home runs. I don't care what people say, nothing is going to give you that gift of hitting a baseball."

After Ralph Kiner signed the ball, I spotted Jeremy Giambi's name on the cart. *Great! He was named the Most Valuable Player (MVP) in the American League last year*, I thought. *I want his autograph!* I asked Jeremy if he would sign a golf ball for me, which he did willingly. As soon as I placed Jeremy's signed ball in my little black bag, I recognized the name of Jason Giambi on another golf cart. I immediately realized that I asked the wrong Giambi for an autograph. Jason Giambi was named MVP, not Jeremy. Who is Jeremy Giambi? I never did follow the Oakland A's that closely, but later on, I discovered that Jeremy played for the A's for three years and was the younger brother of Jason. There's more to this story later in the chapter.

Feeling rather stupid for the mistaken identity, I approached muscular Jason Giambi and politely asked him to sign one of my golf balls. He did, and below his signature he wrote, "MVP 2000."

Four down, four to go.

Joe Torre

"Don't be afraid to fail, encourage your talent, and use your heart."

Right off the bat (no pun intended), I recognized the next celebrity sitting alone in his cart, New York Yankees baseball manager, Joe Torre. A well-respected individual, Joe Torre's record speaks for itself. He led the Yankees to twelve straight playoff appearances in his twelve-year tenure as the Yankees' skipper and won three straight World Series from 1998–2000. Joe also won a World Series ring for the 1994 season. Displaying modesty, he not only signed the Titleist ball but thanked me for asking him to sign. The only other celebrity to thank me was Hal Linden, best known for his

Emmy-nominated role in the TV series *Barney Miller*. I was honored to be in Joe Torre's company, even if it was only for a brief few moments.

Five down, three to go. Surrounded by so many celebrities, I regretted not bringing more balls to the tournament. I needed to be very selective for the rest of the morning, with so many stars mingling around in their new golf outfits.

Vijay Amritraj

"I have been incredibly lucky because I have earned large amounts of money doing what I like best."

I spotted the former Indian tennis player, Vijay Amritraj, practicing on the putting green. At that time, I had no autographs from any of the pro tennis players. Since this event, I have gathered signatures from Jack Kramer, Jimmy Connors, Rod Laver, Pete Sampras, Vic Seixas, and Chris Evert. A longtime tennis player myself, I watched Vijay play many matches in person. The best tennis player to come out of India, he was the top tennis player in Asia for fourteen straight years. Vijay had the perfect tennis body—tall and slim. He looked as fit as ever. Vijay was noted for his great serve-and-volley game and had beautiful classic ground strokes. Vijay won sixteen singles titles and thirteen doubles victories, playing with his brother, Anand. He defeated some of the best, including John McEnroe and Jimmy Connors. Vijay was only too happy to sign a golf ball for my collection.

Six down, two to go.

Rollie Fingers

"In 1971, I had 17 saves and got a raise. In 1985, I had 17 saves and got released."

Although I wasn't an Oakland A's baseball fan, I easily recognized ace reliever, Rollie Fingers, with his famous handlebar mustache. I definitely wanted his autograph. He is the all-time, Major League leader with 341 career saves. Rollie appeared in sixteen World Series games. I'm sure his proudest moment with the A's came when he won the 1974 World Series Most Valuable Player Award with one win and two saves. I cherished the memory of obtaining his autograph.

Seven down, one to go.

Steve Garvey

"You must be passionate, you must dedicate yourself, and you must be relentless in the pursuit of your goals. If you do, you will be successful."

Spying Steve Garvey, I had to have the former Los Angeles Dodgers slugging first baseman's autograph. In person, Steve still projected his "Mr. Clean" image. He was still very muscular and well groomed, as his photos show. I know he gave my San Francisco Giants fits with his great fielding and hitting. After nineteen years in the National League, he retired with a lifetime batting average of .294 in 8,835 at bats. Garvey can also boast of winning four Gold Glove awards. Steve signed my last golf ball—so I thought.

Pat Boone

"I've learned one important thing about God's gifts: what we do with them is our gift to Him."

With no golf balls remaining, I decided to walk around and check out the other celebrities playing in the tournament. So far, no Gregory Peck, but I spotted Pat Boone. He was by far my number one pick for best-dressed celebrity in the tournament. He wore unusual Scottish-plaid knickers with matching socks and cap. I wanted to get a signed ball from the second-most popular singer of the 1950s (behind Elvis). When I was in my early twenties, I was told frequently that I looked a bit like Pat Boone. Maybe it was the fashionable white buck shoes Pat and I wore that made us look alike. Certainly, it was not my looks!

I wanted to ask Pat for his autograph, but I had run out of golf balls. On a whim, I arrived at a clever idea. I asked him to sign on the reverse side of the ball that Jeremy Giambi signed, which he promptly did, and without noticing (as far as I know) Jeremy's signature. It's my only double-signed ball to date, and a great reminder for all autograph seekers to come prepared.

Robert Wagner

"One thing that golf teaches you is humility."

I continued looking for more sports and showbiz celebrities. I didn't have any more balls, but I was still having a ball! I recognized the next famous person near his cart, Robert Wagner, one of the most popular and successful stars in the entertainment industry, and still a handsome man at age seventy. I was very annoyed with myself for not bringing enough balls to sign. A Robert Wagner autographed ball would definitely enhance my collection. His caddie lingered off to the side by himself. I approached the caddie, told him my hard luck story of running out of golf balls, and asked him if he would be kind enough to give me one of Bob's golf balls to be signed by the famous film and television actor. He flatly said no. I whispered a response under my breath, not repeatable. Now what? As I deliberated ways to find just one more golf ball, the second brilliant idea of the day entered my head. *Dummy, you're right there at the driving range. Pick up one of the practice balls.* While no one was looking, I discreetly picked up a range ball that had three stripes on each side with the inscription—Practice. Top Flite, XL 2000.

With practice ball and Sharpie in hand, I walked to Bob Wagner and said, "Bob, I would be grateful if you would sign this golf ball for me. But, there's something I need to tell you. I've run out of golf balls, and I'm sorry I have to ask you to sign a range ball." Bob replied, "You mean you want me to sign a (*expletive*) range ball?" Somewhat shocked, I said, "Not unless you want to sign one of the balls in your bag." Bob stared at me as if I had asked him for the moon, took the range ball, put a very nice signature on it, and gave me a broad smile. Bob Wagner's signed practice range ball displayed in my golf room makes a great story, and all visitors who hear the tale thoroughly enjoy it.

At the Frank Sinatra Celebrity Golf Invitational, I picked up ten autographs on nine balls in a couple of hours. Now, that's what I call having "a great day on the golf course."

I've attended and participated in many charity golf tournaments but have never seen more celebrities in one place than the Frank Sinatra Celebrity Golf Tournament of 2001. The tournament featured more than seventy-two celebrities. Here are some of the other famous people I recognized that day: Yogi Berra, Chad Everett, George Hamilton, Lee Majors, Wayne Newton, Howard Keel, Dennis Quaid, Lou Rawls, William Devane, Dale Robertson, Robert Stack, Dick Van Dyke, Tom Poston, and many more.

All I can say is that Frank Sinatra would be proud to know that his popular golfing event that started out as "Frank's little party in the desert" has become known as one of the most successful charity tournaments in the United

States. It's now called the Frank Sinatra Countrywide Celebrity Invitational. What a nice way to pay tribute to "Ol' Blue Eyes," our nation's first modern entertainment superstar, and his wife Barbara, who is passionate about helping abused children find help and happiness.

However, I never did see Gregory Peck.

CHAPTER 7

THE DONALD

"The most important thing in life is to love what you're doing, because that's the only way you'll ever be really good at it."

As one of the world's most recognizable public figures, Donald Trump is the ultimate definition of the American success story. He began his business career straight out of college by joining his father's New York firm, Trump Organization, focusing on middle-class rental housing. His father, Fred, said of his son, "Everything he seems to touch turns to gold." After studiously learning the company's business for five years, Donald made the big leap into the Manhattan real estate market.

Donald Trump—flamboyant, dynamic, very smart, and often cocky—believes in quality and luxury. This is evident in everything he slaps his name on, including buildings, casinos, hotels, golf resorts, and even reality TV (*The Apprentice*). His grandiose ideas and astute business deals have elevated him to one of the top real estate developers in the world. He once said, "As long as you're going to be thinking anyway, think big."

Donald Trump is a businessman of countless abilities. He wears many hats in his daily life: business executive, entrepreneur, television personality and producer, lecturer, and author, to name just a few of his talents.

At the rate Donald Trump is buying up real estate in New York City—and the rest of the world—he's practically going to own the planet someday. This last statement may exaggerate, but multibillionaire "The Donald" has a passion for real estate and is definitely on a mission. With all of his apprentices, he continues to expand his real estate empire by buying and developing golf courses throughout the world.

An avid golfer—about a four handicap—Donald privately owns, at last count, five golf clubs in the United States and four international golf resorts, with the most spectacular of all soon to be developed. By his own enthusiastic admission, in an interview with the CEO of *Executive Golfer* magazine, the celebrated entrepreneur is planning to build "the world's best golf course in Scotland." Once it is completed, Trump hopes to host a British Open there sometime in the future. A British Open will no doubt take place at Donald Trump's $2 billion golf resort in Menie Estate, Aberdeenshire, Scotland, overlooking the North Sea. Donald Trump has absolutely no doubt that his golf course in Scotland will be the greatest in the world.

Donald Trump has gradually constructed a global golf business through the years, although he claimed in a telephone interview with Hilary Howard (now Hilary Heieck), editor of *NCGA Golf,* Northern California Golf Association's quarterly magazine, that golf comprised only 1 percent of his empire. "Golf has been very good for me, but it's a relatively small section of my business," he remarked.

I saw Donald Trump in person at Pebble Beach during a practice round at the AT&T Pebble Beach Pro-Am in the early part of 2000. His captivating presence drew a large crowd. Tall and stylish, the real estate tycoon finished putting on the third hole, and as he was quickly walking between the ropes, heading for the fourth tee area, I elbowed my way through the mob of jostling autograph hounds to catch him for his autograph. I didn't think I had a chance to obtain it, but I had to try. I was clearly surprised when the New Yorker grabbed the ball from my outreached hand and hastily scrawled his name on it without stopping to get to the next tee. Observing him scribble his name on the ball, I did not expect Donald Trump's autograph to look as prominent as John Hancock's on the Declaration of Independence, but I was hoping the sought-after signature would be somewhat legible. It wasn't. It looked like chicken scratches.

Donald Trump's signed ball displays in a ball rack in my golf room. The only way to recognize "The Donald's" signature is by looking at his printed name beneath the ball. Through the years, I've shown my golf autograph collection to many friends and visitors to my home. Inevitably, someone has commented that Trump's signature looked awful. I've always defended Mr. Trump's penmanship by explaining that he signed the ball while walking and didn't have sufficient time to stop and properly sign it.

A few years later, when my eight-year-old grandnephew commented that he couldn't read Trump's signature, I decided to write a letter to Donald Trump. I explained that the ball he signed for me at Pebble Beach was on display in my golf room, but unfortunately, no one could read his signature because of his illegible writing.

In 2006, I sent the letter, along with the ball to Mr. Trump, congratulating him on the recent birth of his son and on the success of his television show *The Apprentice*. I explained the problem with the golf ball and told him that it would make for a good story if he would sign the same ball on the reverse side, showing the before and after signatures.

I told some golfing buddies how I had returned Trump's autographed ball. A few of them laughed, saying that I took a gamble by returning the ball to him. They figured that I would not get a response from the business magnate, who had more important things to do. They believed that his original signature made for a good story and I should have left well enough alone. I disagreed. My gut feeling told me that Trump, who stands behind everything he does, would understand my concern about his unrecognizable signature and would make it right by signing the ball for the second time.

Within two weeks, my box was returned. I was thrilled to find the original signed ball with his second signature on the reverse side. Although Donald's new signature wouldn't win an award in penmanship, it was recognizable. The second signature resembles the multiple blip lines recorded on a polygraph chart. However, the fact that he honored my request demonstrated his admirable character trait of caring for others, especially my golf collection. He genuinely thought enough of my hobby and love of the game to take the time from his extremely busy schedule to make good on his first signature.

In her telephone interview with Donald Trump, Hilary Heieck asked, "Who is your ideal foursome?" He responded, "Today you always have to say Tiger Woods. He is a spectacular person and a spectacular golfer. He goes to my courses quite a bit. I love Arnold Palmer; he is a special guy. I'd love to bring back the great Ben Hogan in his prime."

In one of Donald Trump's many media interviews, a journalist asked him if the time had come for him to finally slow down a bit, sit back, and enjoy the fruits of his labor. He answered, "Anyone who thinks my story is anywhere near over is sadly mistaken."

CHAPTER 8

PRESIDENTS OF THE UNITED STATES

George H. W. Bush
41st President

"It's amazing how many people beat you at golf now that you're no longer president."

While my wife and I vacationed in Maine in 1991, our itinerary called for a stay in Kennebunkport for a few days. I knew that the forty-first president of the United States, George H. W. Bush, had a summer home in this small seaside tourist town and was a member of the Cape Arundel Country Club. Hoping that I would come face to face someday with former President Bush to get his autograph, I bought a Cape Arundel CC logo golf ball for him to sign, in case our paths crossed. To my surprise, the ball I purchased not only sported the club's logo but also the presidential seal on the reverse side, making the ball more desirable for my collection. All I had to do was acquire George Bush's signature, a very tall order.

My opportunity arose at the AT&T Pebble Beach National Pro-Am in 1993. I knew that President Bush planned to compete in the celebrity tournament, so I called the pro shop to find out what day and time the former president would play a practice round. I drove to Pebble Beach on a Wednesday morning and made certain that I brought the Cape Arundel CC logo ball.

Upon arriving, I immediately went to the practice putting green near the resort's lodge to await George Bush and his entourage. Fans already waited in full force, anxiously looking for a rare glimpse of the former president. In an electric atmosphere, people tightly packed every inch of the ropes around the putting green. The chance to view the one-term president in person created incredible anticipation and excitement among the gallery. The commander in chief during the Persian Gulf War strode down the sloped path toward the green, with a retinue of Secret Service agents hovering around him. The crowd applauded the popular former president as he entered through the ropes to the putting green area. I didn't realize he was so tall. Bush certainly looked presidential.

There's no way I'm going to get close enough to President Bush to ask him for his autograph, I thought. Secret Service agents completely protected Bush; their mission was to ensure the former president's safety. Getting his autograph was practically out of the question. I concluded that solving the Middle East crisis would be easier than getting George Bush's autograph. I never gave this issue a thought when I bought the logo ball on that beautiful New England autumn day in Maine. All I wanted was his autograph for my collection.

I keenly watched George Bush practice his putting before teeing off on Pebble Beach's No. 1 hole. Feeling disappointed that I wouldn't get the autograph, I suddenly got a brainstorm that just might do the trick. It would be a gamble but worth a try.

I pushed my way through the crowd to the entrance of the practice green, where George Bush had to pass to get to the first tee. I noticed no other autograph hounds hanging around; they assumed that getting his autograph was slim to none. However, I was on a mission, and best of all, I had an ace up my sleeve: family connections that went all the way to the top.

My brother-in-law, Major General Lewis Mologne, was commanding officer of Walter Reed Army Medical Center (WRAMC) from 1983 until his retirement in August 1988. WRAMC usually provides annual medical checkups and other treatments to the president and vice president of the United States. Major General Mologne married my sister in 1960, but cancer would claim him just as he retired. At his deathbed, President Ronald Reagan and Vice President George Bush, who both held high esteem for General Mologne, visited him at the Army Medical Center in Washington. They paid their respects and extended their thanks for the thirty-four years of Mologne's honorable service. My sister Rose was on hand to thank President Reagan and Vice President Bush for honoring her husband.

Rose Marie Mologne has maintained her affiliation with WRAMC and is one of the founding members of the Walter Reed Society, a Washington, DC, nonprofit organization established in part to enhance the welfare and the morale of war-wounded servicemen and women returning from Iraq and Afghanistan.

Rose strikes a pose with VP Bush and President Reagan

The tournament's starter announced that George Bush was next on the tee. I carefully kept my eyes on him as he handed the putter to his caddie and proceeded to walk through the entrance of the practice green, where I had strategically positioned myself. Just as one of the tournament volunteers opened the rope to let George Bush pass by, I quickly said to him, "President Bush, you knew my late brother-in-law, Major General Lewis Mologne, at Walter Reed. Would you be kind enough to sign this golf ball for me?" George Bush looked directly at me and said, "Yes, I did." I handed him the ball and Sharpie. He graciously signed it and thrust it in the palm of my right hand. *Oh, no! Not there!*

Whenever someone signs a ball, I always retrieve it with my right thumb and forefinger to make certain the signature doesn't get smeared while the ink is drying. In George Bush's case, I didn't have the chance to carefully handle the newly-signed ball with the Secret Service squad nearly shoving me out of the way to protect the former president. Fearing the worst, I looked at the palm of my right hand and was disheartened to see that some of the forty-first president's signature was smeared on my skin. His signature, of course, was somewhat obliterated, but the "ace up my sleeve" paid off.

On May 6, 2009, eighty-four-year-old former President George H. W. Bush became the ninth person to receive the PGA Tour's Lifetime Achievement Award at the Players championship at the TPC Sawgrass Stadium Course, in recognition of his extraordinary support of the PGA Tour and its players. An honor well deserved.

Gerald Rudolph Ford, Jr.
38th President
"I know I am getting better at golf because I am hitting fewer spectators."

Gerald Ford was the only person to occupy the president's office who had not been elected to the presidency or vice presidency. He became president upon Richard Nixon's resignation.

Among President Ford's favorite pastimes was golf. He was the first sitting president to play in a PGA Tour pro-am, the 1975 Jackie Gleason Inverrary Classic. I was fortunate to watch him play several times in the Bob Hope

Chrysler Classic in the Palm Springs area, where he played for twenty-three years.

At the Bob Hope Classic he picked up the nickname, "The Headhunter," due to conking people on the head with some of his wild tee shots.

Those competing in the Bob Hope tournament, whether they were celebrities or professional golfers, could expect to receive potshots from the famous comedian. No one was spared, not Gerald Ford, or the popular thirty-fourth president, Dwight D. Eisenhower.

Hope fired off these zingers about President Ford. "He's easy to spot; he drives the golf cart with the Red Cross painted on top." "It's not hard to find Jerry Ford at the golf course. You just follow the wounded." Here's my favorite Bob Hope quote aimed at his favorite target. "We have fifty-one golf courses in Palm Springs. He (Gerald Ford) never decides which one of them he will play until after his first tee shot." Although Gerald Ford endured numerous jokes about his errant golf shots, he was a good sport in taking all the ribbing in good humor.

President Eisenhower took his share of teasing from Hope. "Ike loved to paint. I always kidded him that he preferred painting to golf because it required fewer strokes."

Although Gerald Ford bore numerous jokes from Hope about his unpredictable golf shots, he had a few snappy comebacks of his own to the master comic. "In spite of all the wonderful gifts and mementos given to me, if I could have one piece of special memorabilia, it would be the first dollar Bob Hope ever paid on a bet lost on a golf course. The search for that bill wouldn't be difficult. It's still in Bob's right-hand pants pocket."

Former President Ford played in the thirty-eighth (1979) Bing Crosby National Pro-Am and enjoyed playing in the Clambake (probably because he didn't hit anyone). However, he had to holler "Ford" on the first fairway when he right-angled a shot into the trees and barely missed a photographer.

I personally was never able to get Gerald Ford's autograph on a golf ball. However, I knew that he belonged to several country clubs in the Palm Springs area, one of those the gorgeous Club at Morningside in Rancho Mirage, two towns east of Palm Springs. This is Jack Nicklaus's first designed desert course, built in 1981.

I visited the Club at Morningside and spoke to the head pro about getting the former president's signature on a golf ball. Anticipating the pro would do me this favor, I brought along a logo ball with the beautiful American flag stamped on it. Thanks to my connection, the thirty-eighth president signed it!

For the record, I tried to persuade former presidents Bill Clinton, Jimmy Carter, and Ronald Reagan to sign a golf ball for my collection. I was unsuccessful in all three attempts but was pleased to at least receive a reply from all three offices. Although I didn't keep copies of the letters, it's noteworthy to share with you the stories about them.

Jimmy Carter's administrative secretary thanked me for my interest in writing to the thirty-ninth president of the United States but regretted to inform me that the globe-trotting peacemaker signed only historic documents and books.

I was so certain that I would get President Reagan's autograph that I bought a logo golf ball on eBay with the White House seal on it and enclosed the ball in a box with a very personal letter. In the letter, I mentioned that we had met on two different occasions, the first time in 1966 at the Cabana Hotel in Palo Alto, where he gave a campaign speech for governor of California. I explained that after he gave his talk, I walked up to the stage and introduced myself by saying that we were fraternity brothers. I reminded him in the letter that I was a Teke (Tau Kappa Epsilon) at Penn State. President Reagan was a Teke at Eureka College in Illinois.

I also wrote that we met for the second time at the traditional Governor's Breakfast in Sacramento, shortly after he was sworn into office in January 1967. In my job as Public Affairs Manager for Allstate Insurance Companies in Sacramento, one of my duties was to represent Allstate in state governmental affairs. So I attended the breakfast that year to hear Ronald Reagan give his first speech as the new Governor of California.

When I mailed the letter to President Reagan, I knew that he had been diagnosed with Alzheimer's disease. I didn't know how serious his condition was at the time. A few weeks later, I opened my mail and was so excited to find the box I had sent to the former president. Upon opening it, I immediately could see that the special ball had been returned unsigned. A short note inside said that President Reagan could no longer sign his name, because he was severely affected by Alzheimer's disease. I was saddened, not because I didn't get the ball autographed, but because the handwriting was on the wall for a great American with a dreadful disease. He died on June 5, 2004.

I specifically bought a presidential seal logo golf ball on eBay a few years ago to get Bill Clinton's autograph. I sent a very complimentary letter, without the ball, to his New York office in late 2007, hopeful that I would receive an affirmative reply stating that the former president would sign the special ball and telling me where I should send the ball. Instead, I received a very nice eight-by-ten-inch authentic signed photo. Although I'm pleased to have received the signed picture by the forty-second president of the United States, I must confess I was a bit disappointed to not get Bill Clinton's signature on the special ball.

In 2008, I learned that a longtime fellow autograph collector decided to donate three authentically signed presidential balls to my renowned collection—one by Richard Nixon, one by Jimmy Carter, and one by Ronald Reagan on a presidential seal logo ball. I have certificates of authenticity on all three balls.

I also had a double dose of good luck in receiving Bill Clinton's and Barack Obama's autographs from a good friend who was fortunate enough to secure both of these sought-after autographs on balls while they were on the campaign trail during the 2008 presidential campaign.

To my delight, I now have signed golf balls by seven presidents of the United States.

CHAPTER 9

OLLY

"I don't think it's impossible to catch Tiger, but it's close to impossible."

Jose Maria Olazabal gained prominence in the golf world when he captured the British Amateur Championship at age eighteen. He turned pro two years later in 1986, and in his rookie year finished second on the European Tour Order of Merit. Nicknamed "Olly," he has enjoyed success on both the European Tour and the PGA Tour. In his first nine seasons, he finished in the top ten in official World Golf Ranking. Olly came within one victory of the No.1 ranking in the world in 1991. If he had beaten Welshman Ian Woosnam at the Masters, he would have been numero uno. Jose Maria has twenty-eight professional career titles, six on the PGA Tour, including winning two green jackets at Augusta National Golf Club in 1994 and 1999. Augusta National brings out the best in the two-time Masters champion. He also has three other top-five finishes at the Masters. "It's a special place for me. It brings me special memories."

In 2005, I attended the AT&T Pebble Beach National Pro-Am. For some unknown reason, I brought only a three-sleeve of balls for signatures, not prepared for all the possibilities I would encounter that day. PGA Tour pro Andrew Magee and actor/comedian Ray Romano signed balls at Pebble's practice putting green. Ray good-naturedly signed autographs that morning. Always a crowd favorite at the pro-am, Romano demonstrated why "everybody loves Raymond" at the AT&T tournament.

With one ball remaining in my pocket, my goal focused on the two-time Masters champion's autograph, Jose Maria Olazabal. I champed at the bit to get this Spanish golfer's signature to add to my growing collection. I caught up with Jose Maria at Pebble's par-4, sixteenth tee and followed him until he finished playing the famous par-3, seventeenth hole. I knew that I wouldn't be able to get Jose Maria's autograph at the eighteenth putting green because players are protected from fans and autograph seekers and are escorted to a waiting shuttle to transport them to the resort's courtyard entrance. I jumped ahead of Jose Maria on the last hole to walk to the shuttle location, behind the luxury oceanfront suites, overlooking the breathtaking beauty of Carmel Bay. Players accessing the eighteenth green have a choice of walking directly to the shuttle, as most do, or in rare cases, walking up the path in front of the suites leading to the famed Pebble Beach lodge.

My decision to position myself where the shuttle was parked went awry when a security guard, observing that I was there to get autographs, told me that the area was off-limits for autograph seekers and asked me to leave. Taken aback by the security guard's orders, I responded, "Hey, I just want to get one autograph, and I'll be out of here in a flash." The guard, with a furious scowl, threatened to have me escorted from the "sacred grounds" if I didn't leave immediately. I did so begrudgingly.

As I was walking on the roadway, I saw an opening to the course between the oceanfront suites and decided to cut through, in hopes of meeting Jose Maria in case he chose to walk up the path. The security guard who denied me access to the shuttle area must not have trusted me, as his eagle eye watched my every step, including my sudden move to enter the course through the opening. He quickly called the guard stationed at that location and instructed him to escort me out of range of the golf course, which he did very obligingly. Normally, I'm an unflappable person, but not under these circumstances. I was furious, fuming over the treatment by the security guards. Quite honestly, it was very humiliating for me to be chaperoned off the premises for just wanting one autograph. Thank God, there were no onlookers around to witness the embarrassing incident.

Boiling with anger, I remembered an old quotation that put me back in the right frame of mind: *"Follow your bliss, and doors will open up for you."* Now determined more than ever to get Jose Maria's signature, I bravely returned to the side entrance to the lodge and planted myself at the top of the concrete stairs to wait for Jose Maria, in case he decided to walk up the path leading to the lodge. At the top of stairs, another security guard loomed. I thought to myself, *Not again, this can't be happening to me.* However, the guard didn't say a word to me. *Good, he doesn't know I was kicked off the course. I'm safe,* or so I thought.

I waited for what seemed like an eternity for Jose Maria to complete his putting practice. I still had no idea which direction the Spanish golfer would depart from the putting green. After his last practice putt, Jose Maria started walking in the direction of the shuttle, when suddenly he made a turn toward the lodge and headed up the path. I couldn't believe my stroke of luck! I would finally be able to freely ask Jose Maria for his autograph without being harassed. I became so excited that, without thinking, I started walking down the steps leading to the golf course to get closer to Jose Maria. The security guard at the top station shouted, "Stop, you can't go down there!" I said to myself, *Son-of-a-bitch, the guard got a call from "Old Eagle Eye" telling him to be on the lookout for an older man who was after autographs and not to let the person walk down to the course.* Since I didn't want any more trouble, I retreated to the top of the stairs—the neutral zone—and waited for Jose Maria to pass me on his way out.

Getting autographs is supposed to be fun, but it wasn't in this case. I can't remember being so frustrated to get one autograph. As I previously mentioned in the introduction, it took a long time to get Jack Lemmon and Bob Hope to sign balls, but in both cases, I just had to be patient, which is a must for serious autograph collectors. Most autograph seekers would have said the hell with it and given up on getting Jose Maria's signature. Not me. Come hell or high water, I was determined to get his desirable autograph.

My opportunity finally arrived. The Basque player began walking up the stairs. He reached the top landing and started walking toward me. With only the security guard keeping an eye on me, it was just me and Olazabal. When he got five feet away from me, I asked, "Jose Maria, will you be kind enough to sign this golf ball for me?" He answered, "I'm sorry. I don't sign golf balls," and continued walking. I thought, *I must be dreaming. This can't be happening to me!* Reacting quickly as he walked past, I said, "Jose Maria, please, I collect autographs on golf balls as a hobby. I would really like to have your autograph for my collection." He stopped, turned around, and responded kindly, "Since you asked me in such a nice way, I'll do it for you."

I joyfully watched him put a very nice signature on the ball and thanked him for making an exception for me.

At last, I had won my "match" at Pebble Beach!

Jose Maria Olazabal is a classy guy, a fact that emerged at the controversial 1999 epic Ryder Cup match, held at the Country Club in Brookline, Massachusetts. When American Justin Leonard's forty-five-foot birdie putt dropped in on the seventeenth green that ultimately sealed an American victory, the U.S. team went berserk, and a wild celebration ensued, with the U.S. players, caddies, and wives running onto the green to embrace Justin Leonard. The Americans quickly realized that Jose Maria Olazabal had yet to putt and had the opportunity to equal Leonard's score.

The European team expressed anger that the Americans ran across Jose Maria's line of putt, when he had a twenty-five-foot putt that could change the outcome of the match. He missed, to seal his team's defeat. Unlike many of his European compatriots, Jose Maria carried no ill feelings. He said afterward, "I have to say, if it would have been just the opposite, we might have reacted the same way. We're all human beings; we have our emotions. The Ryder Cup brings them to the highest level possible."

CHAPTER 10

ELSIE'S MILLION-TO-ONE SHOT

"Oh, my Lord. It can't be true. It can't be true."

Chico, California, is famous for its agriculture and Chico State College, the second-oldest campus in the California State University system. In the span of a few seconds on April 5, 2007, Chico added another banner when 102-year-old Elsie McLean gained international acclaim overnight as the oldest person in the world to hit a hole-in-one on a regulation golf course. Before I relate her incredible tale, I'd like to share with you some very interesting hole-in-one trivia from the *R&A* (Royal and Ancient) *Golfer's Handbook 2007, Guinness World Records,* and other reliable sources.

Evidence proves that the modern game of golf was played at St. Andrews in Scotland in the early fifteenth century. Golf was the popular sport in Scotland at that time. However, no evidence exists to record the first hole-in-one struck at St. Andrews. For all we know, one of the local shepherds or common soldiers playing a round of golf with a wooden ball might have claimed the honor.

According to the *R&A Golfer's Handbook,* the earliest recorded ace was holed in 1869 at the Open Championship (called the British Open in the United States) by one of the pioneers of professional golf, Tom Morris, Jr., son of Old Tom Morris, golf's first iconic professional figure and famous green-keeper at St. Andrews. The historic ace was accomplished on the 145-yard, eighth hole at Scotland's Prestwick Golf Club, birthplace of the Open.

Until Elsie McLean broke the world record, Harold Stilson from Boca Raton, Florida, was the oldest person to score a hole-in-one. On May 16,

2001, at age 101, Harold entered the record books by recording an ace on the 108-yard, sixteenth hole at the Deerfield Country Club. He aced the hole with a 4-iron.

Who holds the world record for having the most holes-in-one? When you read the answer, you will say, "That's impossible. No mortal can have that many aces." Norman Manley, an amateur player from Inglewood, California, entered the Guinness World Records for carding fifty-nine aces over a span of forty-five years. It is not a misprint or typo: fifty-nine aces! "The King of Aces" scored his first in 1964 and had four holes-in-one in 1979. "I've been called a liar, a cheat, a man with a hole in his pocket," Manley shouts.

Here are three holes-in-one feats that will blow your mind. On July 4, 2002, a Denver professor named Michael Crean made an unbelievable 517 yard hole-in-one on the dogleg par-5 ninth hole of the Green Valley Ranch Golf Club outside Denver. The longest documented hole-in-one on a straightaway golf hole was made by Bret Melson, a student at the San Diego Golf Academy in Hawaii. He aced the 448 yard, par 4, eighteenth hole at the Ko'olau Golf Club in Oahu on February 13, 2007. Until Melson's ace, Robert Mitera was listed in the Guinness Book of Records for having the longest hole-in-one. He blasted a 447 yard drive into the tenth hole of the aptly named Miracle Hill Golf Club in Omaha, Nebraska on October 7, 1965.

It appears that Marie Robie's hole-in-one will stand the test of time. She is listed in the Guinness World Records for achieving the longest recorded ace by a woman. Marie scored an amazing 393-yard hole-in-one in September 1949, at the Furnace Brook Golf Course in Wollaston, Massachusetts.

If Elsie McLean is the oldest person to score a hole-in-one, who is the youngest player to score an ace? Jake Paine was just three years old when he shot his first hole-in-one on a sixty-five-yard hole in Lake Forest, California. Before Jake's ace, a four-year-old lad named Christian Carpenter scored a hole-in-one at the Mountain View Golf Club, Hickory, North Carolina, on December 18, 1999. What about Tiger Woods? He was six years old when he shot his first ace.

Acing a hole is a golfer's ultimate dream and requires skill and lots of luck. It's estimated that forty-two thousand people per year score the rare hole-in-one. Unfortunately, most golfers play entire lifetimes without making an ace. The odds are stacked against the majority of the sixty-five million golfers in the world, of whom thirty-seven million reside in the United States. What are the odds? They vary, depending on many factors, including the skill level of the golfer. *Golf Digest* reported, "One insurance company places a PGA Tour pro's probable chances at 1 in 3,756 and an amateur at 1 in 12,750." *Sports Illustrated* placed the odds at 45,000 to 1 for scoring an ace on a typical par-3 hole. The bottom line? At best, no one knows what the odds are to shoot a hole-in-one. All one needs is the one instant of luck to experience the joy of holing out a tee shot.

One golfer tried to defy the odds of making a hole-in-one. In 1940, Harry Gonder, an American professional golfer, made a twenty-five-dollar bet he could make an ace at his home course, Beverly Shores Country Club, on a 160-yard hole, by continuously hitting balls with the help of caddies teeing and retrieving the balls. He also had two witnesses to count the shots. He gave up after sixteen hours and twenty-five minutes and hitting 1,817 balls. His 1,756th shot struck the flagstaff, but stopped an inch from the cup.

What are the odds of one golfer making two holes-in-one in the same round? One mathematician, Francis Scheid, PhD, retired chairman of the math department at Boston University, calculated the odds at 67 million to 1. With so many golfers in the world, a hole-in-one twice in the same round is not as rare as supposed and has happened on many occasions. To demonstrate how difficult it is to score two aces in the same round, one's chances of winning the Super Lotto are greater, at 41 million to 1.

Holing successive holes-in-one is a different story and considered extremely rare. However, Jack Kendall, sixty-three, from Houston, Texas, had the round of a lifetime in 2006. He accomplished something that no professional or amateur has ever done in the long history of famed Pebble Beach. He aced the 129-yard fifth hole and then drained a pitching wedge from 97 yards on the most famous par-3 hole in the world, No. 7.

Sinking a pair of aces on the same day is an uncommon feat. However, when it comes to acing a par-4, three golfers have shortened the odds beyond reason. Most recently, Paul Harrington, sixty, of Manning, South Carolina, an assistant pro at Wyboo Golf Club in Manning, holed tee shots on the 292-yard, fourth hole at Wyboo, and eighteen days later at the 312-yard, eighth hole at the Dogwood Country Club, Waynesville, North Carolina. The same Norman Manley, who holds the world's record of fifty-nine aces, achieved incredible successive par-4 holes-in-one on August 30, 1964, on the seventh and eighth holes of the Del Valle Country Club, Saugus, California. He shot a course record 61. However, it's doubtful if anyone will surpass Mike Hilyer's unimaginable feat of having ten career aces on par-4s. The six-foot-five former National Long Drive Semifinalist from Orange Beach, Alabama, shot four of them in a fourteen-month period, two of them only five days apart in August 1995. He shot 64 and 63 in those two rounds. At last count, burly Mike Hilyer is still searching for his first ace on a par-3.

If you were told that a father, mother, and son each made a hole-in-one in a three-day span, would you believe it? According to *GolfWorld*, in August of 2007, Gil, Ray, and Sam Mackenzie played a par-3 course in North Wales. Gil made her ace first on the 116-yard, ninth hole. Husband Ray followed up the next day by acing the 115-yard, eleventh hole, and son Sam also aced the eleventh hole on the third day. What are the odds of another family repeating this hat trick? According to bookie William Hill, the chances are ten million to one.

Now here's a hole-in-one story that sounds awfully fishy but was written up in the February 2008 issue of *Golf Magazine*. Christopher Molly, fourteen, carded three holes-in-one in the same round on October 21, 2007, at Shadow Woods Preserve golf course in Bonita Springs, Florida. His father, Ron, witnessed each ace and said, "I know it's like telling someone I just saw a UFO." The odds of three aces in the same round: two trillion to one.

Elmer James and his wife, Marilyn, appear in the Guinness World Records for scoring consecutive holes-in-one on the sixteenth at Halifax Plantation Golf Club in Ormond, Florida, on April 19, 1998.

Personally, I never thought I would score a hole-in-one. After nineteen years of trying, I finally got the monkey off my back on November 20, 2005, on the 172-yard, par-3, eighth hole at my home club, Almaden Golf & Country Club, in San Jose.

Making my first hole-in-one was truly an unforgettable experience for me. What made the ace even more exciting and special was the fact that I was playing with LPGA pro, Wendy Ebster, the 1992 California Women's Amateur champion, who was then Wendy Kaupp. Wendy played on the 1994 U.S.A. Curtis Cup team.

Author (kneeling) shares his first ace with Rick and Wendy Ebster and wife Judy.

In case you're wondering how well the professionals perform in scoring aces, here are some comparisons. The legendary six-time British Open winner, Harry Vardon, who popularized the grip known as the Vardon Grip, still used by most golfers, scored only one hole-in-one in his entire playing life. According to an article in the November 2007 issue of *Golf Digest,* the world's best golfer, Tiger Woods, has eighteen holes-in-one. The champion of champions, Jack Nicklaus, can boast twenty aces. My hero, Arnold Palmer, has nineteen; Gary Player, nineteen; and one the greatest female golfers of all time, Mickey Wright, had eight holes-in-one in her career. Former world-ranked No. 1 golfer, LPGA superstar Annika Sorenstam, whose achievements rank her as one of the most successful women golfers in history, can claim four aces in her golfing career. Michele Wie has had seven with her last one on June 13, 2009.

Here's a Did You Know? Which U.S. presidents have scored a hole-in-one? The answer: Dwight Eisenhower, Gerald Ford, and Richard Nixon.

Nixon supposedly remarked that it was a greater thrill than winning an election.

Here's another test of your IQ. Only a few players have had a hole-in-one on the famous sixteenth at Cypress Point. One was a celebrity singer. Who was he?

A) Andy Williams

B) Frank Sinatra

C) Bing Crosby

D) Dean Martin

Bing Crosby is the correct answer. Playing to a two handicap at one time, Bing can boast of having an amazing thirteen holes-in-one during his lifetime.

The late Bishop John Fulton Sheen, regarded as American television's first preacher of note, said, "Man blames fate for all other accidents but feels personally responsible when he makes a hole-in-one."

Eric Pinkela, golf editor for the *San Jose Mercury*, reported this incredible hole-in-one story in one of his weekly articles. "In the 1989 U.S. Open at Oak Hill Country Club, Rochester, New York, four PGA pros, Doug Weaver, Mark Wiebe, Jerry Pate and Nick Price, aced the 167-yard sixth hole within two hours of each other." According to the National Hole-In-One Association, the odds of four professionals in a field of 156 acing the same hole on the same day are 8.7 million to one.

The late Art Wall, Jr., who won fourteen PGA Tour events, held the record among the professionals for the most holes-in-one. He scored thirty-seven aces during his thirty-one-year professional career, plus another eight in casual rounds. Art's record was surpassed by a Californian who played briefly on the PGA Tour. Mancil Davis is regarded as the world record holder for most holes-in-one by a professional with fifty-one. His first ace came at age 11. By age 13, he had twelve. "They never get old and are always thrilling," said Davis.

You might believe that eight aces in one year would be a record etched in stone. Not so. Dr. Joseph O. Boydstone of Bakersfield, California holds the record for having the greatest number of holes-in-one in a calendar year. He had eleven in 1962.

One of the most memorable and loudest aces had to be Tiger Woods's on the sixteenth hole during the 1997 Phoenix Open at the TPC at Scottsdale. About twenty thousand screaming fans showered the tee with beer cups, cans, and anything they had on them. The roar was so deafening that Tiger's ears were ringing.

Elsie McLean, born in 1904 and a Chico native, using her driver, scored her hole-in-one on the hundred-yard, fourth hole at Bidwell Park Golf Course, a course she's played since 1934. Walking up to the hole, she couldn't find her ball until one of her playing partners found the ball nestled gloriously in the cup and exclaimed, "Oh, Elsie, it's in the hole!" It was her first ace in seventy-three years of playing golf. (Longest wait for first ace: Eight-one years. James Simpson, Dorset, England, got an ace at 89 in 1988). How true is the adage, "It's never too late!"

Chico's suddenly famous 102-year-old resident became the subject of worldwide news and was in high demand to appear on TV and radio talk shows. She initially refused the media invitations, stating that she was weary of the limelight and attention. As she stated, "I'm not used to all this publicity. It's very, very tiring." With encouragement from her daughter, who called her mother's feat a miracle, Elsie finally agreed to make the TV rounds by appearing on the Jay Leno and Ellen DeGeneres shows. Ellen DeGeneres gave her a shiny red golf cart, to which Elsie responded, "I have a golf cart, but this one is so fancy."

A local newspaper reporter asked Elsie, who plays golf regularly at Bidwell Park, what she thought about her remarkable feat. She replied, "For an old lady, I still hit the ball pretty good."

I want to thank my friend, Dick Wilson, from Chico, who plays at Bidwell Park and personally knows Elsie McLean, for getting the spunky centenarian's autograph on a Bidwell Park logo golf ball for my collection. Underneath her name, she wrote 102.

Elsie has celebrated her 104th birthday (she'll be 105 on Nov. 20, 2009) since making her record-breaking ace. She still plays regularly all year around. With a stroke of good luck, Elsie could get her name in the Guinness World Records for the second time—being the oldest golfer in the world. According to the *R&A Golfer's Handbook*, "The oldest golfer who ever lived is believed to have been Charles Arthur Thompson of Victoria, British Columbia.

He shot his age, 103 (a record) at Uplands GC, a course of over six thousand yards. He played on his 105th birthday and died just 107 days short of his 106th birthday in 1975."

Elsie McLean is an inspiration to all golfers and is living proof that playing golf can add years to one's life.

Instant celebrity, Elsie McLean, age 102

CHAPTER 11

MY DREAM 18

A local newspaper reporter covering the story about my autographed golf ball collection asked, "Of all your famous signed golf balls, which ones are your favorites?" I answered, "Good question. No one has ever asked me that question before. I do have a few favorites, but to be perfectly honest, I cherish every autographed ball in my personal collection. Each one has its own story; they're all a part of my family."

After the interview, I started thinking about the reporter's question and decided to write a chapter about some of the autographs that have special significance. I came up with the title, My Dream 18, to feature eighteen (one for each hole on the course) remarkable individuals who have distinguished themselves by either achieving greatness in their professions or finding fame for accomplishing a heroic feat that will live on in the annals of sports. Chapter 11 focuses mostly on PGA Tour greats, but my top eighteen contains an interesting mix of celebrities from other sports and walks of life whose autographs I truly cherish. One of the icons featured in the chapter is the only individual in history to be designated an honorary veteran of the U.S. Armed Forces by Congress.

My Dream 18 autographs do not appear in any special order, with two exceptions. Because he's unquestionably the best golfer in the world and remains the favorite sports star, according to a poll conducted by Harris Interactive, Tiger Woods has the honors on the first tee. My favorite autograph, and the jewel in the crown of my one-of-a-kind collection, appears last. Meet My Dream 18.

FRONT NINE

Tiger Woods

"I want to be what I've always wanted to be: dominant."

Tiger Woods and No. 1 have been synonymous since 2003. Since turning professional in 1996, Tiger's accomplishments predestine him to become the greatest golfer of all time. Tom Watson, the No. 1 golfer in the world from 1978 through 1982, commented on Tiger in the July 11, 2008, issue of *Golf World*, "He's the best who ever played, and I've been saying it for a long time."

Tiger, at age twenty-two, was the youngest player to win the Masters. He also holds the record for the lowest aggregate score at the Masters when he won the 1997 event with 270. The world's highest-paid athlete has the record for holding down the No. 1 position in golf rankings for the greatest number of weeks. His dramatic, sudden-death U.S. Open playoff win at Torrey Pines in San Diego in 2008 marked the five hundredth week that Tiger held the No. 1 ranking in the world. Who can ever forget the 2008 U.S. Open high drama of Sunday afternoon and the Monday playoff? Tiger called it "the most satisfying win of my career."

At the time of this writing, Tiger has won seventy PGA Tour events and needs thirteen more victories to break Sammy Snead's all-time win record of eighty-two official tournaments on the PGA Tour. He needs four more major victories to match Jack Nicklaus' record of eighteen. The legend grows.

In 1995, when Tiger was a member of the Stanford University golf team, I decided to get Tiger's signature on a TPC (Tournament Players Course) at Sawgrass logo golf ball, the course where Tiger won his first U.S. Amateur championship in 1994. I called the TPC pro shop in Ponte Vedra Beach, Florida and bought the ball. Now, I had to figure out how to get Tiger's autograph. I asked my neighbor, Dr. Murray Walker, a member of Stanford GC, to ask his friend, Stanford Hall of Fame golf coach Wally Goodwin, to get Tiger's signature on the ball. Wally, whose team won the national championship in 1994, was able to obtain Tiger's autograph. I also requested that Tiger write beneath his name "1994," the year he won his first national amateur title. The NCAA First Team All-American satisfied my request, making his signed ball all the more unique, especially since Tiger allegedly stopped signing golf balls entirely after he won the 1997 Masters. Having a Tiger Woods authenticated autographed golf ball is a dream come true for an autograph collector because his signature is considered the most coveted autograph in sports.

A picture of Tiger's framed signed ball and the complete story appear in Chapter 15, Tour of Golf Room.

Jack Nicklaus
"The game is meant to be fun."

Jack Nicklaus holds the best record of any golfer in the history of golf. In *Golf Digest's* Fiftieth Anniversary Collector's Edition (July 2000), listing the "Fifty Greatest Golfers of all Time," Jack Nicklaus emerged as No.1. Jack won seventy-three PGA Tour events in his career, eighteen of them major championships, a record that still stands. Jack has the most Masters victories with six. His eighteen majors total twice as many as all but one other golfer, Tiger Woods, who has posted fourteen majors to date. Jack Nicklaus is also the champion runner-up of all time. He has finished second nineteen times and third nine times in major events. Without question, he's a "champion's champion."

It's notable to mention that in 1986, at age forty-six, Jack became the oldest Masters winner in history. Jack shot an incredible six-under 30 on the back nine for a final 65 to win his record sixth Masters victory. He shot eagle-birdie-birdie on Nos. 15, 16, and 17, setting off what is now remembered as one of the loudest gallery roars in golf history. Sports columnist Thomas Boswell, as quoted in *The Gigantic Book of Golf Quotations* by Jim Apfelbaum, said, "Some things cannot possibly happen, because they are both too improbable and too imperfect. The U.S. hockey team cannot beat the Russians in the 1980 Olympics. Jack Nicklaus cannot shoot 65 to win the Masters at age forty-six. Nothing else comes immediately to mind."

Also known as "The Golden Bear," Jack has the most career Grand Slams, having won each major at least three times. Tiger has two.

Jack and I have something in common besides our love affair for the game of golf. We are both Aquarians, sharing the same birthday, January 21st, although I arrived on earth five years earlier. I was fortunate to get Jack's autograph as he walked off the eighteenth green at Pebble Beach in 1990. His autograph became the second signed golf ball in my collection that today totals 221 and counting.

The greatest golfer in the world today, Tiger Woods, commented about Jack Nicklaus, "I think what we remember about Jack is that he's not only the greatest player of all time, but he's a true champion on and off the course. He remains the standard."

Al Geiberger, "Mr. 59"

"People ask me, 'Would you rather have won the PGA or shot 59?'
Of course, ahead of time I would have said the PGA. Now,
I would say the 59 has stuck more."

In the early 1980s, I obtained Al Geiberger's autograph at Silverado Country Club during the Senior Transamerica tournament. Driving home that afternoon, I heard on San Francisco sports radio station KNBR about a unique golf ball that Al Geiberger had given to one of the sports announcers after a morning talk show interview. The logo ball displayed the official scorecard of the 59 that Al Geiberger shot in 1977, at age thirty-nine, at the Danny Thomas Memphis Classic in Tennessee. Al became the first person in history to post a score of 59 (par was 72) in a PGA Tour-sanctioned event. I just had to have this unique ball in my collection and immediately began planning my strategy as I arrived home.

Through a good contact in the California desert where Geiberger once lived, I learned that Al had moved to the Solvang, California, area and played his casual golf at the Alisal Guest Ranch Golf Course. I sent Al a letter, in care of the golf course, telling him what I had heard on the radio station about his special edition logo golf ball and asked if he would sign one for my collection. I enclosed in the returnable box the usual Sharpie pen, stamps, and return labels. I also put a five-dollar bill in the box for the price of the ball.

Within two weeks, when I opened the box, I was pleased to find the unique logo ball hand-signed by Al and surprised to see my five-dollar bill. Al also sent me a small picture of himself kneeling by his golf bag with the official Memphis Classic scorecard in the background. He signed it—Al Geiberger, "Mr. 59"—the same way he signed the unique ball.

If you are curious, Al made six pars, eleven birdies, and one eagle for his then-unheard of 59. His putter was on fire. On the fifteenth hole, which was his sixth because he started on the back nine, he shot birdie, birdie, birdie, birdie, eagle, birdie, and birdie (8-under par in a seven-hole stretch). The gallery was aware he was on track to shoot below 60 and began yelling, "Fifty-nine! Fifty-nine! Fifty-nine!" down the stretch. On his last hole, he had to make a ten-foot putt to shoot the magic number 59. He made the pressure putt and went on to win the tournament.

After shooting the record-breaking 59, Al's kids raced up to their room to tell Mom that Dad shot a 59. She said, "Fifty-nine what?"

"Mr. 59" won eleven PGA Tour events, including one major, the 1966 PGA Championship. His second PGA victory came in 1963 at the Almaden Open Invitational, the country club where I am a member. Al also had ten wins on the Senior PGA Tour.

Since he shot the first 59 in 1977, three other PGA Tour and LPGA players have recorded golf's magic number 59. Chip Beck was in the zone, in 1991, when he carded a 59 at the Las Vegas Invitational; David Duval had to eagle the finishing eighteenth hole (Palmer Course) in the final round of the 1999 Bob Hope Chrysler Classic at PGA West in La Quinta, California, to shoot a 59; and Annika Sorenstam became the first LPGA pro to shoot a 59 at the Standard Register Ping event in Arizona in 2001. Annika birdied the first eight holes en route to her record 59. I witnessed David Duval's 59, and I have signed balls from all four members of the exclusive "Club 59." I must ask: Who will be the first pro to shoot a 58? Tiger Woods? For the record, Tiger has shot two 61s and a pair of 62s in tour-sanctioned events.

For his historic 59 on June 10, 1977, Al Geiberger will forever be known as "Mr. 59."

Mickey Wright

"When I play my best golf, I feel as if I'm in a fog, standing back watching the earth in orbit with a golf club in my hands."

Born in San Diego, Mickey Wright has been praised as the all-time greatest woman golfer. The Associated Press named her the Greatest Female

Golfer of the Twentieth Century. Harvey Penick, one the greatest instructors in the history of golf, proclaimed in his 1992 *Little Red Book,* that Mickey was the greatest woman player of all time. Betty Hicks remarked in our interview that Mickey Wright was the best female golfer she had ever seen. One of golf's all-time great champions, Ben Hogan, said, "Mickey's swing was the best I've ever seen, man or woman." Kathy Whitworth, who won eighty-eight official LPGA Tour events during her storied career—more than any woman or man—remarked in her instructional book, *Golf for Women,* "Of all the players I've watched, men and women, nobody could swing a golf club as well as Mickey Wright. In her overall game, she was just head and shoulders above everyone." LPGA Hall of Famer Betsy Rawls said of Mickey, "I always say Mickey was the best golfer the LPGA ever had. I think most of the people who ever saw her play still think that. The public flocked to see her because she was so spectacular."

Mickey won eighty-two LPGA Tour events, including thirteen majors, placing her second on the all-time win list behind Kathy Whitworth. "Mickey could have won a hundred tournaments if she hadn't quit early," Whitworth said. Mickey Wright was only thirty-four when she retired in 1969, due to health problems. Mickey still holds the record for the most victories in a five-year span. From 1960-64, Mickey won fifty tournaments. She also holds the record for the most LPGA wins in a season, thirteen in 1963. She accomplished the career Grand Slam by the age of twenty-seven.

Mickey was inducted into the LPGA Hall of Fame in 1967. Besides gladly signing her name on the Stanford logo golf ball (as a Stanford alumna) that I had mailed to her, Mickey wrote *HOF 1967* on the ball, making it even more special. I'm proud and honored to have in my collection a hand-signed ball from one of the greatest woman golfers of all time, smooth-swinging Mickey Wright.

Willie Mays

"Every time I look at my pocketbook, I see Jackie Robinson."

Who is the greatest baseball player of all time? It all depends upon the age of the person you're asking. If my now deceased father answered, he would have replied Babe Ruth, along with many other baseball fans who say The Babe was the greatest player in the history of baseball. In a 1969 ballot commemorating the one hundredth anniversary of professional base-ball, Babe Ruth was named baseball's greatest player ever. Fans from my generation, 1950 to 1970, believe that Willie Mays was the greatest baseball player of all time.

I never saw Babe Ruth play baseball, but I watched Willie Mays for his entire career, beginning in 1951 when he joined the New York Giants. Nick-named the Say Hey Kid, Willie became the best all-around baseball player in history. He could hit with power, run with speed, and had a super arm. The great Joe DiMaggio always noted that Willie Mays had the greatest throwing arm in baseball. Willie was regarded as the best center fielder in history. The unforgettable over-the-shoulder catch that he made near the wall in Game One of the 1954 World Series has been replayed many times on film. The Giants swept the Cleveland Indians in four games. The series is best remem-bered for "the Catch."

Willie Mays finished his career with 660 home runs, placing him fourth behind Barry Bonds' 762, Hank Aaron's 755, and Babe Ruth's 714. Many smart baseball writers note that if Willie hadn't spent two years in the Army, from 1952 to 1953, and not played half his games in one of the coldest and windiest ballparks in the country, Candlestick Park, he might have held the all-time home run record. Willie admitted that his only regret in base-ball was not breaking Babe Ruth's home run record. "That's the only thing I wanted to do that I didn't do," he said.

The best athlete to wear number 24, Willie appeared in twenty-four All-Star games, a major league record. Willie was asked one time who he thought was the best player he had ever seen during his playing days. He replied, "I don't mean to be bashful, but I was."

Bobby Thomson

"Can you imagine, I hit one home run and people still remember?"

October 3, 1951, is a moment frozen in baseball history. I was a sopho-more in high school. On that day, my eyes were glued to the classroom wall clock, anxiously waiting for the school bell to go off at 3:45 p.m. to end classes. When the bell rang, I dashed out of the classroom and ran home two blocks, hoping to watch the televised final National League playoff game between the New York Giants and the Brooklyn Dodgers for the National League pennant. I was a die-hard Giants fan, as I proudly proclaimed in "How I Became a Collector."

Arriving home in record time, I immediately turned on the TV set, unsure if the game was still on. Much to my dismay, I learned that it was the bottom of the ninth inning and the Dodgers were ahead 4 to 2. With knots in my stomach, I thought, *It's going to take a miracle for my Giants to win the game and pennant.* The Giants had two men on base, one out, and a great hitter coming to the plate—Scotland-born Bobby Thomson, a feared hitter. I knew a home run would win the game, but I would settle for the Scotland Flash getting a single or a walk, because on deck was twenty-year-old rookie sensation Willie Mays, an even bigger threat at the plate. Dodgers manager Charlie Dressen made a pitching change and brought in ace reliever Ralph Branca (who has contributed to my autograph collection), a three-time All-Star, to relieve starting pitcher Don Newcombe (his autographed golf ball was donated to my collection). Bobby stepped up to the plate and took a called strike. At 3:58 p.m., the next pitch, a smoky fastball, was thrown, and the rest is history. Bobby Thomson hit an electrifying three-run homer into the lower left-field stands, and veteran Giants play-by-play announcer Russ Hodges began his famous twenty-one-second repeating scream. "The Giants win the pennant! The Giants win the pennant! The Giants win the pennant!" Hodges supposedly yelled "The Giants win the pennant!" eight times. When I witnessed the "Shot Heard 'Round the World," Bobby's blast was immortalized in my mind and certainly became my most exciting moment in the history of baseball. I'll never forget it! I'll never forget it! I'll never forget it!

Former Giants great Bobby Thomson came to San Francisco in 2001 for the fiftieth celebration of his most famous home run. A newspaper article mentioned that Bobby resided in Watchung, New Jersey. I called the Watchung Chamber of Commerce, told them about my golf autograph collection and asked for his home address. Frankly, I was surprised the Chamber voluntarily gave me his address. I sent a letter to Bobby, told him I'd been a Giants fan all my life and had watched him hit his famous three-run homer at the Polo Grounds. I politely asked if he would sign a Giants logo ball for my one-of-kind collection. Shortly thereafter, I received a note telling me to send the ball and he would sign it. He returned it signed with a short note thanking me for my loyal support of the Giants.

Gene Sarazen

"The more I practice, the luckier I get."

Bobby Thomson wasn't the only person to hit "the shot heard 'round the world." Gene Sarazen's double eagle (known as an albatross), in the 1935 Masters, created a worldwide stir, but there were only about two dozen witnesses to Gene's feat. In the final round, he holed out his miraculous second shot from 225 yards, with a four-wood over water, giving him a two on the par-5, fifteenth hole, forcing a playoff. Gene won the thirty-six-hole playoff (the only one in Masters history) the following day. His double eagle is arguably the most famous shot in golf history. Gene called it "just a piece of luck."

What are the odds of making a double eagle? Some have estimated six million to one. No one knows for sure what the correct figure is, but it's clear that the double eagle is the rarest feat in golf.

Known as "The Squire" for his elegant style and fashionable knickers, Gene Sarazen was born Eugenio Saraceni. After reading his name in the newspaper after his first professional win, he didn't like it because the name reminded him of a violin player and immediately changed it. He once remarked, "I don't care what you say about me. Just spell the name right."

Gene Sarazen is famous for more than his double eagle. In 1930, he invented the modern sand wedge, calling it the sand iron. Gene was also the first golfer to win a "career" Grand Slam, in that he won the U.S. Open and British Open, the PGA Championship, and the Masters during his career. No golfer has ever captured all four modern Grand Slam events in the same year. Tiger Woods is the only golfer in history to win four consecutive majors, winning the last three in 2000 and claiming the Tiger Slam when he won his second of four Masters in 2001. Thus, the Tiger Slam is regarded as one of golf's most incredible achievements. Only three other PGA Tour golfers in addition to Gene Sarazen and Tiger Woods have won a career Grand Slam— Ben Hogan, Gary Player, and Jack Nicklaus.

One of the most beloved figures in golf history, Gene Sarazen was among the first class of inductees into the World Golf Hall of Fame, in 1974.

On vacation in Marco Island, Florida, in 1992, I read in one of the golf magazines that Gene Sarazen lived on the island. Wanting to have his autograph for my collection, I obtained his address from his home golf course and sent him a ball to sign. I was thrilled when I received the signed ball, dated 1992. He was then ninety. At the time of his death, at age ninety-seven, Gene Sarazen was the oldest member of the PGA of America.

Ben Hogan

"As you walk down the fairway of life, you must smell the roses,
for you only get to play one round."

My first autographed golf ball came from Arnold Palmer, and Jack Nicklaus signed the second ball in my collection. Who would be next? I thought of several legendary golfers, but in truth, I wanted the immortal Ben Hogan's autograph next. The problem was that Ben Hogan had retired from competitive golf in the early 1960s, and where would I have a chance of seeing him in person to ask for his renowned signature? I had one option and decided to try it. I wrote a letter to *Sports Illustrated,* telling my story of collecting autographed golf balls and practically pleading with them to send me Ben's home address. Somebody must have felt sorry for me, or it was the luck of the Irish. I received a letter from *SI* with Ben's home address. I wrote Mr. Hogan, explaining that I regretted never having the pleasure of watching him play in person and ended the letter by saying how much it would mean to me to have his famous autograph in my private collection. I sent him one of his own manufactured balls—the 392LS Hogan 4. I got lucky. He signed it. Why was Ben Hogan's autograph so important?

Besides winning nine majors and sixty-three PGA Tour victories, ranking him fourth among all-time winners behind Sam Snead, Jack Nicklaus, and Tiger Woods, Ben Hogan is regarded as the best ball striker the game has ever known. Hogan invented practice. He became addicted to practicing, and he would hit balls until his hands bled. The golf pros followed him just to watch his ball-striking ability. The late PGA Tour Hall of Famer Tommy Bolt said of Ben, "He's the only player I have ever known to get an ovation from the fans on the practice tee. I've seen him playing practice rounds before a tournament, and half his gallery was made up of other professionals." Someone asked Jack Nicklaus if Tiger Woods was the best ball striker he had ever seen. Jack responded, "No, no, Ben Hogan, easily." Even nine-time major champ Gary Player always said that Ben Hogan was the best ball striker from tee to green that he ever saw.

Ben's influential book *Five Lessons: The Modern Fundamentals of Golf* is in its sixty-fourth printing. This classic golf instruction book is still considered the "bible" for aspiring professionals and by most golf teachers.

In researching the Texan golfer, nicknamed "The Hawk," I learned that Ben Hogan was responsible for arranging the Champions' Dinner at the Masters. In 1952, as defending champion, Ben hosted a dinner for the past winners, and the Champions' Dinner became a fixture. Here's another interesting piece of information that makes for a good trivia question. Who's the only player to have won the Masters, the U.S. Open, and British Open in the same calendar year? Gentleman Ben accomplished the feat, known as the "Hogan Slam" season, in 1953.

I wasn't the only hound after Ben Hogan's autograph. One of golf's fine PGA Tour players and colorful personalities, Peter Jacobsen, asked Ben for his autograph at the 1990 Colonial National Invitation by saying, "Mr. Hogan, would you please sign my visor?"

How feared was Ben Hogan in competition? Here's what legend Sam Snead had to say about Ben. "I'm only scared of three things: lightning, a side hill putt, and Ben Hogan."

Hogan once commented, "Golf is not a game of good shots. It's a game of bad shots."

Ben Hogan's name will live on as long as the game of golf is played. In 1987, Ben was asked how he would like to be remembered. He replied, "I would like to be known as a gentleman first, and next as a golfer. That's all."

Sam Snead

"Until you play it, St. Andrews looks like the sort of real estate you couldn't give away."

Omitting Sam Snead from My Dream 18 list is like excluding Michael Jordan from playing on the original U.S. basketball team that won the gold medal in the 1992 Summer Olympics. He is the all-time leader in PGA Tour wins, with eighty-two. Sam is credited with 135 worldwide victories, including seven majors. The U.S. Open was the only major he didn't capture, although he finished second four times. Sam won tournaments in six decades, winning his first event in 1936 and last in 1982. Although he wasn't the oldest professional golfer to better his age, Sam Snead was the first golfer to shoot his age on the PGA Tour. In 1979, age sixty-seven, Sam shot a final round 66 at the Quad Cities Open. At age fifty-two, he won the 1965 Greater Greensboro Open, making him the oldest player to win a PGA tournament. In 1983, at age seventy-one, the iconic Sam Snead shot a phenomenal 60 at his home course in Virginia to beat his age by eleven strokes.

I remember seeing Sam Snead in the 1950s when he appeared on a television show called "You Asked for It," hosted by Art Baker. The weekly TV program resembled a believe-it-or-not show where viewers could send in odd, curious, strange, and unusual requests. For example, one viewer wanted to see $1 million dollars in one-dollar bills. Another time, a viewer wanted to see the vaults at Fort Knox, where the majority of U.S. gold is kept. One viewer read in a golf publication that PGA Tour golfer Sam Snead claimed he could par any golf course in America using only a 5-iron. The viewer wanted to see Sam Snead prove it by playing his country club course, Tam O'Shanter, located near Chicago. Show host Art Baker read the request and then announced, "Because you asked for it, here's Sam Snead at Tam O'Shanter Country Club playing the course with only a 5-iron in his hands." In a ten-minute segment of the program, Snead used his 5-iron off the tees, fairways, and putting greens, making par on every hole and the course, thus fulfilling the inquiring viewer's request.

In 1995, I drove to the desert to watch the Liberty Mutual Legends of Golf tournament held at the famed PGA West Stadium Golf Course in La Quinta, California. I was thrilled to see in person many of the great golf names of the past: Arnold Palmer, Sam Snead, Tommy Bolt, Art Wall, Jr., Gene Littler, and Don January, to name a few. These six super golfers won a combined total of 272 PGA Tour and Senior Tour victories. I already had Arnie's signature and was able get four of the other five old-timers to sign a ball that morning at the driving range, except for Sam Snead. I came to the tournament primarily to see Sam Snead in the flesh and obtain his autograph. Unfortunately, I missed getting his autograph at the driving range, as he was quickly shuttled to the tenth hole, where he started his round. I thought, *No problem, I'll get his autograph after he finishes his round at the ninth hole.*

I decided to follow Snead, who was regarded as having the perfect swing in golf. "The most fluid motion ever to grace a golf course," said Jack Nicklaus. Sam's electrifying appearance drew a large gallery, as he was certainly the marquee player of the tournament. Born in Virginia, Sam, age eighty-three, wore his trademark straw hat. He earned the nickname Slammin' Sammy for wowing the galleries with his long drives. He lived up to his billing that day when he drilled his opening tee shot long and straight down the tenth fairway. He received a warm applause, smiled, and tipped his hat.

I followed Slammin' Sammy for six holes. Each time he walked onto the tee, the fans cheered in appreciation for what Sam Snead meant for golf. I was very impressed with his graceful swing and his entire game from tee to green. In my eyes, Sam Snead lived up to his legendary fame as one of the most dominant golfers in the history of golf.

I followed many of the other legends during the day, but I made sure that I was at the ninth putting green when Sam Snead finished his round. Unfortunately for me and all the other autograph hounds hanging around to get Slammin' Sammy's autograph, we couldn't get close enough to ask the Virginian golfer for his autograph, as he quickly walked straight into the Stadium's clubhouse to turn in his scorecard.

Not one to give up easily, I lingered around the front entrance of the clubhouse, in case the legend walked out of the building. I saw a legend emerge, but he wasn't Sam Snead. He was Art Wall, Jr., the PGA Player of the Year in 1959, the same man who signed a golf ball for me earlier in the day at the range. I knew that Art was born in Pennsylvania and at one time held the PGA Tour record for the most holes-in-one with thirty-seven. I approached Art and thanked him again for signing the golf ball in the morning. When I told him that I grew up in the Pittsburgh area, he was very friendly and happy to spend a little time talking with me. He was impressed that I knew about his career total of thirty-seven holes-in-one. I told Art that I collected autographs on golf balls for a hobby and mentioned my disappointment in not being able to get Sam Snead's autograph during the day. Art kindly said,

"I can help you get Sammy's autograph. Come with me." Someone up there must like me.

I followed Art into the Stadium's clubhouse, and we went directly into the player's locker room. Imagine my excitement and thrill when I came upon the great Sam Snead sitting on a bench about to change into his street shoes. Art walked up to his good friend and said, "Sam, this man collects autographs on golf balls. I told him that I would help him get your signature on a ball." Sam said in a folksy tone, "Why does he want my autograph?" I wasn't sure if Sam was joking or not, so I jumped in on the conversation and said, "Mr. Snead, your autograph would mean so much for my collection. I'd be honored to have your signature on a golf ball." Sammy must have liked my answer because he graciously signed it. I thanked him and gave Art a warm handshake for helping me acquire an autograph from one of the greatest golfers of all time. Sadly, Sam Snead and Art Wall, Jr., have passed away, but my memory of these two legends will live on forever.

BACK NINE

Jack Kramer

"Tennis is the only sport where a champion can go on forever being a piece of equipment."

I can't leave off my Top 18 list the name of Jack Kramer, my boyhood idol, who is regarded as one of the greatest tennis players of all time. My first tennis racket was a Jack Kramer Autograph. Not only was this the most popular racket in the '50s, it was also the best wood tennis racket ever made. I won my first tennis tournament at age eleven with a JK woody.

When I took up the sport in the '40s, Jack Kramer was ranked No. 1 in the world and held that ranking for a number of years. Jack won twelve Grand Slam tournaments, including Wimbledon three times and nine U.S. Championship titles. Few people know that Jack Kramer was the first man to win Wimbledon in shorts. He won the British tournament that year in 1947 in a breeze, losing only thirty-seven games, a record that still stands.

I read in an NCGA magazine article that the Northern California Golf Writers Association honored Jack for his dedication and support of golf.

I didn't know that Jack Kramer played golf until I learned that he owned a golf course in the Los Angeles area called Los Serranos Country Club. I went online and got the club's address and sent Jack a letter telling him that he was my boyhood idol and that I watched him play when he toured the country. I sent Jack a unique yellow golf ball that resembled a small version of a tennis ball. Jack not only returned the unique ball signed, but also sent me a signed Los Serranos CC logo ball. Now that's what I call a class act.

Jack Kramer will always be remembered as the man who made professional tennis respectable. When I think of Jack Kramer, I always will remember my first tennis racket and all the matches I won with it.

Byron Nelson

"Golf is a lot like life. When you make a decision, stick with it."

When Byron Nelson passed away at age ninety-four in 2006, he was the last link to a bygone era of golf. Legend Byron Nelson will be remembered for many reasons, but mostly for his fabled eleven consecutive PGA Tour victories, an all-time record, and a total of eighteen wins out of thirty tournaments that he entered in 1945. Byron's 1945 season is the best ever by a male golfer. His streak of eleven straight wins is considered among the most untouchable records in all of golf. I place it on par (no pun intended) with New York Yankee Joe DiMaggio's fifty-six-game hitting streak in 1941.

Byron won fifty-two PGA Tour events in his short career. Had he not retired at the early age of thirty-four to become a rancher, Byron undoubtedly would be alongside Sam Snead, Jack Nicklaus, Tiger Woods, Ben Hogan, and Arnold Palmer in total PGA Tour victories.

I regret not being able to witness Byron Nelson play golf in person. Mr. Nelson will be remembered as one of the all-time best golfers and one of the most gracious players to ever play the game. He was a true gentleman on and off the course.

Most of today's professional golfers don't know that in winning the U.S. Open in 1939, Byron became the first champion to wear a short-sleeved, open-necked shirt. In the same tournament, his 1-iron into the hole from two hundred yards is still considered the greatest single shot in U.S. Open history.

Byron Nelson was a member of the TPC Four Seasons Resort and Club at Las Colinas, Irving, Texas, where the Byron Nelson Championship takes place each year. I was able to get a fellow Texan Allstate manager (a member of the club) to get Byron's autograph on a golf ball, in the early 1990s.

The late Bryon Nelson received the nation's highest civilian award, the Congressional Gold Medal of Honor, in June 2007. His wife warmly accepted the award on his behalf.

Payne Stewart
"Not that money is a driving force. It's an honor to play for your country."

I feel fortunate to have a Payne Stewart autographed golf ball in my collection. He loved America. As he once said, "I'm one of those people who place my hand on my heart when they play the national anthem. Heck, I sing the words."

Besides winning eleven PGA tournaments, including two U.S Opens and a PGA Championship, Payne Stewart won six international events. People considered his golf swing one of the best on the PGA Tour. Payne was probably the most recognizable golfer in the world because of the unique clothing he wore. He always stood out on the course, wearing tam-o'-shanter caps with coordinated knickers and socks.

In Chapter 3, I mention that I attended the 1991 AT&T Pebble Beach Pro-Am with my very good friend Roger Dennis and his son Danny. I started out by watching the pros at Poppy Hills because I knew that Payne Stewart would be there practicing with his celebrity partner. We caught up with Payne at the sixteenth tee box and followed him from there. An unfortunate incident happened after Payne putted out on the short par-3 seventeenth hole. As Payne was walking between the ropes to the eighteenth tee, I asked him for his autograph. Much to my surprise and shock, his celebrity partner stepped in front of me and said, "Don't bother him. He's practicing." I thought to myself, *What right does Payne's partner have to tell me I can't ask Payne for his autograph? If Payne didn't want to sign the golf ball, I'm sure he would have told me.* Payne walked past me without acknowledging my request. I followed him to the eighteenth tee. While Payne was waiting to tee off, an unknown man walked up to me and said, "Do you want Payne's autograph?" I said, "Yes, but how are you going to get it when I was just turned down by his celebrity partner?" The stranger said, "I'm Payne's father." I'm sure he witnessed the incident and felt sorry for me. I happily handed the ball to Payne's dad and watched him go over to his son who took the ball and signed it. When Payne's father returned the ball to me, I couldn't thank him enough for his thoughtful gesture. It wasn't until a few years later, when reading the *1994 AT&T Pebble Beach Pro-Am Supplement*, that I learned that Payne Stewart's father was deceased. The stranger who told me that he was Payne's father turned out to be his "second dad," Jim Morris, a Springfield, Missouri, insurance man who was a close friend of Payne's late father, Bill Stewart.

Sadly, Payne Stewart and five others were killed in a tragic airplane accident on October 25, 1999, when his Learjet flew uncontrolled, until it ran out of fuel and plunged into a South Dakota pasture, four hours after it left Orlando, Florida on a flight to Texas. The cause of the crash remains unsolved, although it appears the Lear 35 had a sudden loss of pressurization.

I have many fond memories of Payne Stewart. I'll never forget the incident at Poppy Hills in getting his autograph. I can still see Payne jumping up, screaming in celebration after his fifteen-foot putt disappeared into the eighteenth cup to win the 1999 U.S. Open at Pinehurst, beating Phil Mickelson by one shot. It seemed like he and his caddie were never going to stop hugging each other.

I'll never forget Payne's very moving memorial service where pro golfer and close friend, Paul Azinger, came up to the pulpit to offer his eulogy. Paul stood there for a moment, and to the surprise of the three thousand people in attendance, he put on a tam-o'-shanter cap, rolled up his trousers as if he was wearing knickerbockers and gave a poignant tribute to his very close friend. "Payne Stewart loved life."

A month after his death, I watched on television as twenty-one of his friends on the PGA Tour opened the 2000 U.S. Open by simultaneously hitting balls into the ocean at Pebble Beach, a twenty-one-ball salute.

A quote by Payne Stewart sums up his pleasant attitude about life. "But in the end, it's still a game of golf, and if at the end of the day you can't shake hands with your opponent and still be friends, then you've missed the point."

Annika Sorenstam
"I believe in positive thinking."

There's a very simple reason Annika Sorenstam made my Dream 18 list. Her record-breaking achievements rank her as one of the most successful and dominant female players in golf history. With an amazing seventy-two LPGA Tour career victories, including ten major championships and another eighteen victorious tournaments internationally, her total ninety victories worldwide make her the female golf player with the most wins to her name. Annika won LPGA Player of the Year a record eight times, including five straight seasons. The Swedish-born golfer ranks third on the LPGA all-time victory list, behind Kathy Whitworth (88) and Mickey Wright (82).

In name recognition, Annika ranks in the top five in professional golf, along with Tiger Woods, Arnold Palmer, Jack Nicklaus, and Michelle Wie. She is the only female golfer to have shot a 59 in competition. "Ms. 59" accomplished this feat in the second round of 2001 Standard Register Ping event at the Moon Valley Country Club in Arizona.

The first time I had the opportunity to get Annika's autograph on a golf ball was at the 2004 Nabisco Dinah Shore LPGA event, held each year at the Mission Hills Country Club in Rancho Mirage, California. As much as I tried, I couldn't shove my way through the mob to catch her for her sought-after signature, and she didn't stick around long enough to satisfy all the autograph hounds like me.

My big chance to get this true golf legend's autograph came at the 2008 Samsung World Championship, held at the Half Moon Bay Golf Links in Half Moon Bay, California. Luckily, a friend who lives at the course gave me a pass that permitted me to enter the course grounds the day before they allowed the public in to watch the pro-amateur event. After following 2007 World Championship winner Lorena Ochoa and getting my picture taken with her, I met up with Annika and her caddy on the first tee. She was practicing by herself and graciously signed the ball. The following day, my wife took a picture of Annika and I, after she completed her round in the pro-am. She signed the picture on Sunday, October 5, 2008, after her last professional round of golf in Northern California. The signed photo by Annika is priceless.

On May 13, 2008, Annika announced to the world she would retire at the end of the year. "I think I've achieved more than I ever thought I could," she said during a news conference at the Sybase Classic in New Jersey. "I have given it all, and it's been fun. I'm leaving the game on my terms," she said.

Author and Annika

Joe Montana

"There's no thrill like throwing a touchdown pass."

The consensus is that Baltimore Colt Johnny Unitas was the greatest pro quarterback of all time. For me, my pick for the best QB was San Francisco 49er, Joe Montana. Both quarterbacks grew up in my neck of the woods, the Pittsburgh, Pennsylvania, area. Nicknamed "Joe Cool," *Sports Illustrated* in 2006 rated Joe Montana the No. 1 clutch quarterback of all time. Joe was also nicknamed "The Comeback Kid" for a good reason. He led the 49ers to an astonishing thirty-one fourth-quarter, come-from-behind wins. Joe began his NFL career in 1979 with the 49ers. He can proudly boast that he started in four Super Bowl games, and the team won all of them. He will always be remembered for his last-minute touchdown pass to his favorite receiver at that time, Dwight Clark, to bury the Dallas Cowboys in the NFL Championship Game in 1982. That famous play will always be known as "the Catch." Not surprisingly, the winning touchdown came at the end of a ninety-two-yard drive.

I was able to get Joe Montana's autograph on a 49er logo golf ball at Stanford University's practice range, where he would often practice and play at Stanford. Joe's autograph is one of my favorites.

Bob Hope

"If you watch a game, it's fun. If you play it, it's recreation.
If you work at it, it's golf."

I am thrilled to have a signed ball from one of the most admired celebrities of all time, Bob Hope. I have so many fond memories of Bob Hope appearing in Hollywood films and on television, entertaining our troops while wearing Army fatigues, as a show of support for our military. No one has done more for our men and women in uniform than Bob Hope. I can still see Bob at Christmastime, on stage with a golf club in his hand, cracking his famous one-liners as he entertained the soldiers abroad. In 1997, an act of Congress made Bob an Honorary Veteran. Bob said, "I've been given many awards in my lifetime, but to be numbered among the men and women I admire most is the greatest honor I have ever received."

It took me over two years to get Bob Hope's autograph. I met his publicist, the late Ward Grant, in 1991 during the Bob Hope Chrysler Classic. I told Ward that I collected autographed golf balls for a hobby and asked him if he would get me Bob's autograph. He said yes and to send him the ball. I got his address and sent him a Palm Springs logo golf ball. Periodically, I dropped a note to Ward, reminding him of my request, and finally after two years, I received the signed ball in the mail with a short note from Grant saying that Bob Hope signed the logo ball on his ninetieth birthday. I wish the comedian had written ninety underneath his signature, which would have made the ball all the more special, since the Palm Springs desert icon had his sixth hole-in-one in 1993 in Palm Springs at the age of ninety.

Bob Hope was always good about signing autographs. Supposedly, he would sign up to 350 autographs a day off the golf course. One time, someone asked him for his autograph at the urinal in the men's room. He told the man, "Pal, if you'll just let me finish, I'll sign it for you."

The English-born American was an avid golfer who took up the sport in the 1930s and, with the help of Ben Hogan, Bob worked his handicap down to a four for a short time. He found so much humor in golf and came up with many great and clever quotes. Here is my favorite Bob Hope golf quote. "Golf's a hard game to figure. One day, you'll go out and slice it and shank it, hit into all the traps, and miss every green. The next day you go out, and for no reason at all, you really stink." No one has done more to promote the game of golf and to raise money for worthy charitable causes than Hollywood treasure Bob Hope. He was inducted into the World Golf Hall of Fame in 1983.

Bob, thanks for the memories.

Gary Player

*"If there's a golf course in heaven, I hope it's like Augusta National.
I just don't want an early tee time."*

In writing this chapter about the world's most traveled athlete, Gary Player, I learned this South African-born golfer ranks first in total professional victories with 163 worldwide. He is arguably the most successful international golfer of all time. Gary claims that he has flown over fifteen million miles since turning professional as a seventeen-year-old and has spent the equivalent of four years sitting in an airplane. What PGA player can boast that he is the only player in the twentieth century to win the British Open in three different decades, 1959, 1965, and 1974? The answer: Gary Player. He's also proud to claim that he played the most British Opens and Masters.

I'm sure one of his proudest moments in golf came in 1965, when he completed the career Grand Slam of Golf at age twenty-nine, joining Gene Sarazen and Ben Hogan. Tiger Woods won the career slam in 1999, at age twenty-four, making him the youngest to complete the slam. Player is the only golfer to have won career Grand Slams on the PGA and Champions Tour.

I was fortunate to have met and talked with the fit South African golfer at the Silverado Country Club at one of the senior events. Not only was he nice enough to autograph a golf ball for me, he also let me pose with him for a picture. Without question, Gary is golf's international ambassador.

Can you imagine playing in the Masters once? Five times? Twenty times? Gary Player, at seventy-three, called it a career at the Masters after his fifty-second Masters in 2009. He holds the record for the most appearances. The first foreign-born Masters champion, Gary played his first Masters in 1957 and won the green jacket three times—1961, 1974, and 1978. When two-time Masters winner Phil Mickelson was asked what he thought about Gary Player's longevity in the game, he replied, "The level of golf he's played for so many decades is staggering."

Gary can also blow his horn for being the first U.S. Open winner (1965) to be neither British nor American. He's also regarded as the best bunker player the game has ever known.

Dubbed Mr. Fitness, Gary Player has, at last count, put his signature on over 300 golf courses throughout the world. I'm sure there's one course he wished he had designed, his favorite, Cypress Point in California, ranked second in *GOLF Magazine's* Top 100 Courses in the U.S. for 2008. He was inducted into the World Golf Hall of Fame in 1974.

There's simply no getting around it. Gary Player is one of a kind. The game of golf has grown immensely thanks to this great golfer and wonderful family man. He, like Chi Chi Rodriquez, remains one of golf's best showmen, and sad to say, there aren't too many of them left.

Author and Gary Player

Lorena Ochoa

"It always feels good to be a little ahead of the players."

Since 2007, the new face of the Ladies PGA Tour and the pride of Mexico is Lorena Ochoa.

Born in Guadalajara, the eight-time Mexican National Champion began playing golf at age five. She won five consecutive Junior World Golf Championship titles. She is the first Mexican golfer of either gender to be ranked No.1 in the world.

Lorena attended the University of Arizona on a golf scholarship and won the NCAA Player of the Year Awards for 2001 and 2002. She turned professional after her sophomore year at the university. Her golf coach at the University of Arizona, Greg Allen, said, "As good as Lorena Ochoa is at golf, she is ten times as good a person off the course. Everyone who has ever encountered Lorena loves her."

I found her coach's statement to be so true, in the few times I came face-to-face with this classy golfer who has held down the No. 1 spot in women's golf since April 2007. The first time I met Lorena was in 2007, during a practice round at the Longs Drug Challenge at Blackhawk Country Club in Danville, California. I decided to catch up with the Mexican star at the ninth putting green for her autograph. As I arrived, several Mexican groundskeepers were waiting for Lorena to finish the hole and thank her for buying their lunch for the entire week. I told one of the workers I was there to get Lorena's autograph on a golf ball. He said, "Stay here with us because I'm sure Lorena will stop by to say hello before going to the next hole." In fact, she did stop. Lorena signed the ball and agreed to have my picture taken with her. She later signed the photo at the 2008 Samsung World Championship, where I had the chance to talk privately to her during a practice round. I can understand now why everyone loves Lorena Ochoa.

Lorena has won twenty-six victories on the LPGA Tour at print time. She owns two major titles, capturing the 2007 Women's British Open at the historic Old Course at St. Andrews and the Kraft Nabisco Championship in 2008. Lorena played her way into the record books when she became the first woman to earn more than $4 million in a single season in 2007.

Upon winning the Corona Championship in Mexico in 2008, Lorena qualified for her sport's greatest honor, the LPGA Hall of Fame. The most beloved figure in Mexico, Lorena has to be on tour for ten years—in her case, until 2012—to be eligible for induction. "It was very special to do it here in my home country," Lorena said.

Arnold Palmer
"Winning isn't everything, but wanting it is."

If I had to pick out just one autograph that stands out from all others in the collection, it would be Arnold Palmer's. The date of October 25, 1989, is frozen in my mind. It was on that day that I saw Arnie in person for the first time in my life. He also on that date signed my first golf ball, which launched my autographed ball collection, which changed my life for the better.

Chapter 1 was devoted to this man, who needed no introduction. I would like to add a quote from today's greatest golfer, Tiger Woods, who after winning the $7 million Tour Championship in Atlanta on September 16, 2007, was told he needed one more win to tie Arnold Palmer for fourth place in all-time PGA Tour victories. "He's the king," Tiger said, "to even be in the same breath as Arnold Palmer, you know you've done something special."

My Dream 18 autographs from my collection are dreams come true for me. If you had the opportunity to play a round of golf with three of these eighteen or any other celebrities, who would make up your dream foursome? I based my selections on the time when they played in their prime. Arnie for his "go for broke" competitive nature and for popularizing the game of golf. Tiger because I would like to be able to say that I played with one of the greatest, if not the greatest, golfer of all time. My third pick may surprise you. I would like to see what the greatest golf swing of all time would be like, and that's why I'd be honored to have sweet-swinging Mickey Wright in my dream foursome. Who would comprise your dream foursome?

CHAPTER 12

IN A CLASS BY THEMSELVES

We've all heard the age-old axiom, "records are made to be broken." Is there such a thing as an unbreakable record? In my opinion, yes! Here are six records that will never be matched.

1. Coaching major college football the longest at a single institution.
(Sixty years as of 2009)

Joe Paterno
"The name on the front of the jersey is what really matters, not the name on the back."

As a Penn State alumnus, I must mention the name of one of the most renowned college football coaches of all time, Joe Vincent Paterno. As of the 2008 season, eighty-two-year-young "JoePa," as he's affectionately known, had 383 victories to his credit, ranking him No. 1 in victories among major college coaches. The living legend also holds the Division I record for the most undefeated seasons in college football history.

After graduating from Brown University in 1950, where he played quarterback and cornerback, Brooklyn-born Paterno hired on at Penn State as an assistant coach, at age twenty-three. He succeeded Hall of Famer Rip Engle as head coach in 1966.

It's hard to believe the five-time National Coach of the Year has been at Penn State since Harry Truman was in the White House. Coach Paterno would love to see a college playoff system, but knows he probably won't be around to see it happen. In his own words, "I'm only going to be head coach another ten to fifteen years, and I don't think it will happen by then."

Here's a brainteaser. Who holds the record for the most bowl victories?

A) Woody Hayes (Ohio State)

B) Knute Rockne (Notre Dame)

C) Bobby Bowden (Florida State)

D) Joe Paterno

If you picked "D," you are correct! Paterno has twenty-three bowl wins out of thirty-five postseason appearances. He's also the only coach to have won the "Grand Slam" of football: Rose, Orange, Fiesta, and Sugar Bowls. Penn State has also won eleven other different bowl games, including winning the Cotton Bowl twice.

Joe Paterno's Nittany Lions have won two national championships, in 1982 and 1986. Penn State has registered seven undefeated regular seasons, which is why JoePa has long been an advocate of a college football playoff system. Joe Paterno was inducted into the College Football Hall of Fame on December 4, 2007. He would have joined Bobby Bowden and John Gagliardi of Saint John's University as the first active coaches to be inducted in 2006 had it not been for the knee injury he sustained at the Wisconsin game in 2006. A new rule change by the National Football Foundation grants eligibility to any coach over the age of seventy-five, instead of post-retirement.

How sought after is JoePa's autograph? One of the Oregon State football players stated that win or lose, after the September 2008 game between Oregon State and Penn State, he wanted to get JoePa's autograph after the game. I hope he got it. I got mine by writing to the already-immortal coach at Happy Valley, the frequent nickname for State College, Pennsylvania. JoePa had many reasons to smile in 2008; his team won the Big Ten Conference and he was named Big Ten Coach of the Year.

Many know Joe Paterno as the feisty coach who paced the sidelines (before his injury) constantly during games, wearing his trademark khakis with his cuffs rolled up above his black sneakers. Yet his influence extends well beyond the white chalk lines of the football field. Despite devoting his life to college football, he believes that education should always come first. I remember him stating in an interview many years ago that if he had his way, college freshmen would not be eligible to play varsity football. He felt it was wrong that a varsity freshman could play football before setting foot in his first classroom. He believed that freshmen should be red-shirted, as permitted under NCAA rules. I'm sure he still feels the same way about freshmen football players, but he has no choice but to play exceptionally talented freshmen to remain competitive.

Although best known for his love of football, the generosity of Joe Paterno and his wife Sue is well known within the Penn State community. To date, their charitable contributions to Penn State have totaled more than $4 million.

Joe Paterno is truly one of the great college football coaches of all time. Pete Carroll, University of Southern California (USC) head football coach, universally regarded as one of the top college football coaches in the country, said, "Joe Paterno is a classic. Joe is remarkable, simply remarkable. To be that tough for so long, to endure so much, to stay in one place and keep winning, he's a once-in-lifetime coach."

Is it time for the "winningest," most active, top-tier football coach to retire? Nope. In fact, JoePa just "re-upped" for three more years, taking his reign through the 2011 season. And every year Joe Paterno continues to coach, it becomes clearer that his record of coaching major college football the longest at a single institution will stand as long as there is college football. Of that, there is absolutely no doubt. As acclaimed sports author John Feinstein so eloquently wrote in the January 19, 2009, *Sporting News* magazine, "Enjoy Joe Paterno while you can. You won't see the likes of him again."

2. College football's all-time winningest coach (461 wins as of 2008)

John Gagliardi
"Call me John, not coach."

Along with Joe Paterno's autograph, I also had to have a signed ball, obtained by mail, from America's "winningest" football coach, whose last name matches mine. His name is John Gagliardi (pronounced Guh-Lahr-Dee). When my grandfather came to America from Italy in the 1880s, everyone in the "new country" pronounced his name "Gag-Lahr-Dee," a phonetic butchering that must have frustrated many immigrants. Grandpa Raymond didn't like hearing his name mispronounced and became tired of correcting people. To make it easier for everyone to correctly pronounce his name, Grandpa dropped the second "g" in his last name.

John Gagliardi, eighty-two, the legendary head coach at Saint John's University in Collegeville, Minnesota, has 461 wins on his resume and ended his sixtieth season in 2008 as a collegiate head football coach and fifty-sixth season as head coach at Saint John's. He has won four National Championships, named national coach of the year eight times, and became the first active coach to be inducted into the College Football Hall of Fame in 2006. John has been able to field great football teams because he has created a unique coaching style, one he calls, "Winning with No's." No calling him coach, simply call him John; no lengthy calisthenics; no tackling during practice; no laps; no long practices; and no swearing. He relates to his kids and gets them to play hard. Saint John's is in Division III football with no scholarships. At St. John's, you play for the love of the game and also for the love and respect for John Gagliardi.

John has no immediate plans to retire from coaching. When asked about his job security at the Benedictine school, he was quoted in *Sports Illustrated*, "The monks give me a lifetime contract. But if we start losing games, they can give me the last sacraments and declare me dead." When John finally retires from coaching football, his career win numbers will for sure stand the test of time and never be broken.

The two greatest coaches, JoePa and John

3. All-time record of eighty-eight LPGA wins.

Kathy Whitworth
"No one ever conquers golf."

Few golfers know that Kathy Whitworth won eighty-eight LPGA tournaments, which is the all-time record among men and women. Her closest competitor, Mickey Wright, won eighty-two times, matching icon Sam Snead's wins on the men's side.

Kathy was born in Texas but reared in New Mexico. She eventually took up golf at age fifteen. A natural athlete, Kathy quickly showed promise of eventual stardom and came under the wing of Harvey Penick, a golf teacher in Austin, Texas, who eventually taught many professionals. In his *Little Red Book*, Harvey wrote, "There's no nicer person on earth than Kathy." Harvey knew he had a prize in Kathy, who arrived for lessons already possessing a good and natural shoulder turn. He only had to change her grip and follow-through. She went back home and won the New Mexico Amateur, and her golfing career took off.

Kathy's first LPGA Tour victory came at the 1962 Kelly Girl Open and won her last title in 1985 at the United Virginia Bank Classic. The lanky Texan was the first woman to win $1 million, reaching that goal in 1981. Among her many awards and honors, Kathy was selected Associated Press Female Athlete of the Year in 1966 and 1967, winning seventeen tournaments in those two years. It is not surprising that Kathy holds the LPGA record for most holes-in-one in a career with eleven.

Kathy Whitworth is listed in *Golf Legends of All Time*, published in 1997, that honors the seventy greatest golfers who ever picked up a club.

Kathy, after having a successful career on the LPGA Tour, authored her first book, *Golf for Women*, in 1990, based on her many years of playing and teaching at golf clinics. When my wife Judy started taking golf instruction in the early 1990s, her teacher advised her to buy *Golf for Women,* an easy-to-read instruction book for women golfers of all skill levels. I sent the book to Kathy, who lives in Texas, and requested her autograph to add to my book collection. She graciously signed the book, "To Joe, Best always, Kathy Whitworth," and returned it to me with a hand written note that read:

Dear Joe,

This is hard to believe, but my dog ate your return envelope. So I hope this gets to you as your address was chewed up as well. Best always, Kathy Whitworth.

Kathy Whitworth's eighty-eight LPGA wins is a record so unbelievable in women's professional golf that there's simply no chance it will ever be broken.

4. Most yards gained (22,895) in professional football.
5. Most receptions (1,549) in professional football.
6. Most touchdowns (208) in professional football

Jerry Rice
"What you saw out there on the football field was an individual who loved the game."

Former San Francisco 49er Jerry Rice is widely regarded as the most prolific pass receiver in pro football history. Some sports writers have said that Jerry Rice is the greatest football player ever. Born in Mississippi, the NFL football legend's statistics are so dominant that he's in a league of his own. At last count, the *Dancing with the Stars* celebrity holds thirty-eight career records, most notably career receptions (1,549), yards gained (22,895), and touchdowns (208). With certain induction into the Pro Football Hall of Fame in 2010, Jerry was selected thirteen times to the Pro Bowl and owns three Super Bowl rings.

In 2007, *Golf Digest* released its ranking of the top hundred golfers from the world of sports using official USGA handicaps. Jerry was one of the notables on the list. He was nearly a scratch golfer. The legendary football superstar played to a low of .8 handicap index. A friend (Jerry's caddie) was able to get Jerry to sign a unique San Francisco 49er logo ball that resembles a football at one of the AT&T Pebble Beach Pro-Am tournaments. He inscribed his uniform number, 80, beneath his name.

In an interview with Hilary Heieck, editor of *NCGA Golf*, Jerry was asked, "If you had the opportunity to play with three others to make up your dream foursome, who would you choose?" He replied, "Arnold Palmer, Jack Nicklaus, and Payne Stewart." Having second thoughts, Jerry added, "And I have to include Tiger Woods."

Without a doubt, Jerry Rice's three records (yards, receptions, and touchdowns) will never be eclipsed. They're etched in stone. The best receiver of all time has his name printed into almost every passing category in the annals of professional football.

I also have autographed golf balls from other superstars whose records, in my opinion, are untouchable. They are:

1. Cal Ripken's consecutive starts of 2,632 baseball games.
2. Bret Favre's NFL record of most career passing yards (65,127), most pass touchdowns (464), and most completions (5,720).
3. Byron Nelson's eleven consecutive PGA Tour wins and eighteen total victories, in 1945.
4. Tiger Woods making 142 tournament cuts in a row, from 1998 to 2005; winning fifty PGA Tour victories by age thirty; and scoring average of 68.17, in year 2000.
5. Chris Evert's career win-loss record (.900) in tennis singles.
6. Steve Young's NFL career quarterback rating of 96.8.
7. Jim Brown's most seasons led NFL in rushing: eight.

Other superstars from my roster of autographed golf balls may have records that will never be broken due to new changes in sports rules and multitudes of great new talent. Who knows? However, the records listed here are not likely to be eclipsed.

CHAPTER 13

NOTABLES

In addition to the fifty-one professional golfers and celebrities featured or mentioned in the first twelve chapters, I've collected golf ball autographs from many other sports and showbiz personalities whose claims to fame are indisputable. The superstars listed alphabetically have truly earned a berth in this chapter for these most notable reasons.

Name	Claim to Fame
Troy Aikman	Considered among the best NFL quarterbacks of all time
Marcus Allen	Became NFL's first player to rush for over 10,000 yards and catch passes for 5,000 more
Notah Begay	First full-blooded American Indian professional golfer
Seve Ballesteros	Former World No. 1 golfer, won two Masters and two British Opens
Rick Barry	Only player ever to lead the NCAA, NBA, and ABA in scoring
Tom Brady	Holds NFL record for most touchdowns in a single season (fifty)
Jim Brown	Generally considered the best running back of all time

Sir Bob Charles	First lefty to win a major (the Open) and knighted by the queen
Fred Couples	Former World No. 1 American professional golfer
Sean Connery	Rose to fame portraying secret agent *James Bond 007*
Jimmy Connors	World No. 1 tennis player for 160 consecutive weeks (1974-1977)
Paula Creamer	At eighteen years, nine months, she is the young est winner of a seventy-two-hole LPGA event
Ben Crenshaw	One of the greatest putters in the history of golf
John Denver	One of the world's best-known and best-loved folksingers
David Duval	Only PGA golfer to shoot a 59 in the final tourna ment round
Pete Dye	A legend in the field of golf-course design
Ernie Els	Held No. 1 spot in golf's world ranking
Julius Erving	"Dr. J," the dominant basketball player of his era
Chris Evert	Her career win-loss record (.900) in singles is the best in tennis history
Nick Faldo	Europe's most successful golfer and winner of six majors
Bret Favre	Holds the NFL career passing touchdown record (442)
Bob Feller	Threw three no-hitters, including the only open ing day no-hitter in 1940
Harrison Ford	Ranked No. 1 in *Empire's* "The top 100 movie stars of all time" list
Dan Fouts	Holds NFL record of averaging 320 yards passing per game
Lou Holtz	Only coach in NCAA history to lead six different teams to bowl games
Julie Inkster	Second oldest LPGA player to win two majors after turning forty

Hale Irwin	Won U.S. Open three times and leading winner on Champions Tour
Tony Jacklin	Most successful United Kingdom player of his generation
Bo Jackson	First athlete to be named an All-Star in two major sports
Samuel Jackson	The highest grossing actor of all time
Magic Johnson	Rated the greatest NBA point guard of all time by ESPN
Michael Jordan	The greatest basketball player in history
Rod Laver	Only tennis player to win the Grand Slam twice
Mario Lemieux	First man to win the Stanley Cup as a Penguins player and then as its owner
Nancy Lopez	Greatest female golfer of her generation
Ronnie Lott	Considered one of the best defensive backs in NFL history
Tony LaRusso	First baseball manager to win multiple pennants in both leagues
John Madden	His winning percentage (.750) is the best of any coach in NFL history
Andrew Magee	Had the first hole-in-one on a par four in PGA history
Dan Marino	First quarterback to ever pass for five thousand yards in a season (1984)
Casey Martin	PGA Tour golfer who rode a cart to the U.S. Supreme Court and won
Phil Mickelson	Greatest left-handed professional golfer of all time
Johnny Miller	His final round of 63 is the lowest round ever shot in a U.S. Open
Jack Nicholson	Most nominated male movie actor in Academy Award history
Greg Norman	"The Shark" was the world's No. 1 ranked golfer in 1980s and 1990s

Barack Obama	The first African-American to be elected president of the United States
Corey Pavin	Holds the PGA record for the fewest number of strokes in nine holes (twenty-six)
Michael Phelps	The first athletic to win eight gold medals at a single Olympic game
Cal Ripken, Jr.	Baseball's Iron Man played in a record 2,632 straight games
Brooks Robinson	Sixteen-time Gold-Glover with Baltimore Orioles and All Century Team
Luc Robitaille	Highest-scoring left wing (LA Kings) in NHL history
Bret Saberhagen	Won the American League Cy Young Award in 1985
Pete Sampras	Fourteen Grand Slam titles, six years consecutively No. 1 in tennis
Roz Savage	Attempting to become the first woman to row alone across the Pacific Ocean (SF to Australia)
Don Shula	Won more games (347) than any other NFL coach
Vijay Singh	Ranked No. 1 golfer in the world for thirty-two weeks, in 2004 and 2005
Leon Spinks	Won world heavyweight title in 1978, upsetting Muhammad Ali
Louise Suggs	One of founding members of LPGA in 1950
Vinny Testaverde	Holds the NFL record for throwing TD passes to 70 different players
Joe Theismann	As Washington Redskins' quarterback, he was NFL's MVP in 1983
Tom Watson	Only player to win British Open on five different courses
Eric Wright	Among select group of SF 49ers who owns four Super Bowl rings
Chuck Yeager	First pilot to fly faster than the speed of sound
Steve Young	Holds four NFL records, including highest career QB rating, 96.8

CHAPTER 14

TRICKS OF THE TRADE

Collecting sports autographs is one the fastest growing hobbies in the world today. For me, it's been an exciting and deeply satisfying pastime. Although I'm not in the business of collecting golf autographs for money, my extensive collection has appreciated in value over the years. The thrill of the hunt and the joy of meeting celebrities in person and getting their autographs give me the greatest satisfaction. It's my passion!

If you decide to collect autographs, it's important to know that you won't hit a home run every time you ask a celebrity for an autograph. Although my personal collection contains more than 260 autographed items, some professional golfers say no when asked to sign a golf ball. Baffled by this situation, I asked popular Champions Tour player Peter Jacobsen why he believes some pros won't sign golf balls. "I don't have any issues with signing autographs, but some guys get very funny about it. Some don't sign balls. Why? I can't figure that one out. Some say they don't want the ball to end up on eBay! I say, so what?"

If you decide to buy an autographed item on eBay or any online seller, be very savvy and cautious about what you're buying, because there are unscrupulous individuals offering desirable autographs to unwitting buyers at bargain prices. The biggest red flag is the deal that sounds too good to be true. Experts in the sports memorabilia field claim that 50-75 percent of the autographed pieces for sale are forged.

Many honest dealers and sellers thrive in the autograph business, and some share proceeds with worthy causes. In order to ensure that you're dealing with a reputable seller, buy from vendors who are members of organizations such as the Professional Autograph Dealers Association or the Universal Autograph Collectors Club. I belong to the Golf Collectors Society. If in doubt, ask the seller which association he belongs to and contact the organization to find out if the person is a member in good standing. A reputable dealer gives a money-back guarantee or a Certificate of Authenticity.

One of the most popular and least expensive ways to collect autographs is by mail. However, I find the most enjoyable way to collect autographs is in person. Not only do you meet famous people up close and in person, you also get guaranteed authenticity of the autograph.

I've been collecting famous signatures since 1989 and have picked up some of the "tricks of the trade" along the way. As a salesman at one time, I learned how to handle rejections. I converted some rejections into autographs by knowing what to say and having a never-give-up attitude. Following are a few examples:

Harding Park Golf Course in San Francisco, named after the twenty-ninth president, hosted the WGC-American Express World Golf Championship in 2005. Padraig Harrington, Ireland's leading golfer, played a practice round in the Championship. As he approached the fifth tee box, I politely asked the Dubliner, before about fifteen spectators, to sign a golf ball. He flatly told me that he didn't sign golf balls and kept walking. Reacting quickly, I said loudly enough for everyone to hear, "What if my grandparents came from Ireland?" The twenty-four-year-old Irishman turned around, shot me a look, and walked over to where I stood behind the roped-off area. As I handed Paddy the ball and Sharpie, he took a pen out of his pocket and signed the ball in green ink. At that moment, the onlookers clapped and cheered, something I've never experienced in my twenty-plus years of collecting autographs. I got that ball by thinking fast and using my sales "tools," such as heritage, connections, and not taking a no for an answer.

Padraig Harrington was voted PGA Tour player of the year by his peers for 2008, becoming the first European player to win the award since it began in 1990. His two major wins (British Open and PGA Championship) in 2008 have most likely opened the door to the Hall of Fame.

In 1998, the U.S. Open was held at the Olympic Club in San Francisco. After following Tom Lehman and Lee Janzen (the eventual winner) for a few holes, I decided to catch up with the 1997 British Open champion, Justin Leonard. I positioned myself to the side of the fourteenth tee box while he finished up practicing on the previous green. As soon as he entered the roped off fourteenth tee area, I said, "Justin, would you be kind enough to sign this golf ball for me?" "I don't sign golf balls," he responded. "Please," I pleaded. Justin slowly walked toward me, stopped, glared into my eyes, and told me once again in a very nice way that he didn't sign golf balls. With about a dozen spectators listening intently to the interaction taking place between the two of us, I asked for the second time in the most sincere voice, "Pleaseeeeeeeese." My perseverance and determined plea changed his mind. The hero of the 1999 Ryder Cup match came over, took the ball and signed it. Happy with my accomplishment, I thanked him very much. Again, persistence paid off. You don't have to get pushy to get your autograph, just be nice and say please.

Most professional golfers will sign golf balls if you catch them at the right time and right place. Early in my career of collecting autographs, I asked Senior PGA golfer George Archer to sign a golf ball during a practice round at Silverado Country Club in Napa, California. He said, "I don't sign golf balls." A year later, an announcement in the *San Jose Mercury* noted that George Archer, winner of twelve events on the PGA Tour including The Masters in 1969, would make a signing appearance at a San Jose retail golf shop. Even though he had told me that he didn't sign golf balls, I gambled by going to the shop to try once again for his autograph. As I entered the store on a Saturday morning, I was surprised to find so many people waiting in line to get an autograph from this very tall golfer (six feet six inches). I must admit that I was a little nervous when it came time for me to ask George to sign my golf ball. I thought, *What the heck, all he can say is no.* Wearing my suit of armor, I asked, "George, will you please sign this ball?" He showed an entirely different personality off the course. This time he responded, "Absolutely." Never give up! It's a good motto to live by.

Acquiring the autograph of Dave Stockton, a two-time PGA champion and winner of fourteen Champions Tour events (including the 1996 U.S. Senior Open) was another triumph that could have gone awry. Judy and I were attending the Transamerica Senior tournament at Silverado Country

Club. Toward the end of the day, we headed for Silverado's beautiful, historic main mansion, a popular hangout for the pros and spectators. I spotted Dave Stockton leaving the players' dressing rooms and heading for the mansion. As one of the best putters on the Senior Tour, Stockton's autograph was worth its weight in gold. Judy and I both approached him. I asked for his signature, and he quickly remarked, "I don't like to sign golf balls." I could have responded, "Dave, that's your prerogative and thanks just the same." Instead, I bluntly asked, "Why?" "It makes my handwriting look terrible," Stockton replied, grinning broadly. His smile tipped me off that he would sign the ball, which he autographed very neatly.

Some pro golfers sign only certain golf balls due to a clause in their sponsor contract. When I approached Brad Faxon, an eight-time winner on the PGA Tour, for his autograph at Pebble Beach, he asked, "Is it a Titleist ball?" I looked and replied no. He said, "Sorry, I can only sign Titleist golf balls." I almost asked him if he would sign one of the balls in his bag for me but decided that would be too bold.

The following year, I got Brad to sign a ball at Pebble Beach because I came prepared with a Titleist ball. I reminded him what happened with my request the year before, and the Rhode Island resident was only too happy to sign the ball. Brad Faxon is considered one of the best pure putters in golf history. When asked his secret in putting, he explained his success this way, "My only secret is confidence. I just try to hit every putt as if I've just made a million in a row."

Here are some suggestions to novice autograph seekers for getting golf autographs. These tips have worked very well for me.

1. **It's important to know when and where to ask for the autograph.** Practice rounds (Monday through Wednesday) are the best days to get your favorite golfers and celebrities to sign items. On Wednesdays, the pros and celebs will typically be at the course practicing and participating in the pro-am event. Try to go as early as possible to catch the pros before they enter the driving range. Another good time to get pros to sign is after practice rounds. Champions Tour player Scott Hoch had this to say in the April, 2007 *Golf Digest* article, "How to Get Your Favorite Golfer to Sign Something." "After practice rounds is the best time. We all have our little routine before a round and don't like to be disrupted." Try your luck in getting autographs at the

practice putting green, where many of the pros and celebrities finish up the day. Don't ask for autographs once the tournament begins. PGA Tour rules forbid pros to sign autographs during competition (Thursday through Sunday), until the round is completed. Although the pro-am celebrities are not supposed to give autographs during tournament play, some do in order to honor a spectator's keepsake request.

2. Know something about the pro. Utilize your knowledge of the pro and personalize the request in a specific way, demonstrating that you are a true fan. As an example, when I approached the woman golfer ranked No. 1 in the world, Lorena Ochoa, for her autograph in 2007, I congratulated her on the banner year she was having on tour. I told her that she was "a cinch to be named LPGA Player of the Year for 2007." She smiled, thanked me, and happily signed the ball. As she handed the ball back to me, I said, "Muchas gracias, sonorita." She responded, "De nada." The twenty-five-year-old from Guadalajara, Mexico, even took the time to have her picture taken with me, which makes her Numero Uno in my book.

Author and Lorena at Blackhawk Country Club

3. Be sure to carry a permanent marker with you. I prefer the Fine Point Sharpie marker for getting a well-defined, durable signature. A word of caution: handle the pen with care and if you use a Sharpie, allow the ink to dry for at least fifteen seconds or so to prevent smearing of the signature.

4. **Consider asking the golfer to use your name.** Although I haven't felt the need to do this, golf pro Scott Hoch recommends asking the player to make the autograph out to your name, as the golfer may be more likely to sign because he or she won't think you're going to sell it on the Internet. The chance of an autograph being genuine is greater if the collector asks that the item be autographed to him or her personally such as well-liked PGA Tour player Jim Furyk did for me at Pebble Beach: "Joe, Best Wishes! Jim Furyk." The pros are getting wiser these days and can smell the collectors or dealers who make money off signed items from eBay. "Players are very hesitant to sign for these guys," said pro Peter Jacobsen. "Sometimes, they pay young boys and girls $1 to go get the autograph for them, knowing some players will never turn down a cute eight-year-old."

5. **Collecting autographs through the mail.** Chances are you won't be bumping into someone like Tiger Woods on the street, but with a little effort, obtaining autographs by mail can be easy and inexpensive. I've gotten quite a few autographs this way. If you go this route, be original. Personalize your letter by saying something other than, "I'm your greatest fan!" Also, if you are sending an item to be signed, always include the proper sized postage-paid envelope or box. When I can't get a golf ball signed in person, I always send a small returnable box with ball, a nice letter, Sharpie pen, return label, and proper postage stamps determined by the post office. I'm batting .800 (twenty out of twenty-five) this way. The last autographed golf ball I got through the mail came from John Madden, former head coach with the Oakland Raiders, a Hall of Famer.

6. **Send your request to the PGA or LPGA Tour and they will forward it to the golfer.** Scott Hoch, a winner of eight PGA victories and three Champion Tour wins, said in the *Golf Digest* article mentioned in tip No. 1, "If all else fails, send a request letter to the PGA Tour. They'll put it in my box, and I'll mail autographs on my own time."

7. **Ask your friends to help you get autographs.** For example, my very good friend and golfing buddy, the Reverend Kenny Foreman, founder of the Cathedral of Faith church in San Jose, knew that I collected autographed golf balls. He was able to get Evander Holyfield to sign a ball for me, after

the four-time heavyweight champion of the world gave his testimony at the church one Sunday. The champ wrote beneath his name Phil. 4:13, the Bible chapter meaning, "I can do all things through Christ who strengthens me." Pastor Foreman also obtained for me a signed ball by American country singer, Randy Travis. It never hurts to get a little help from your good friends.

8. Always show respect for the celebrity. Pro golfer Peter Jacobsen summed it up best by these remarks e-mailed to me, "If you're asking for an autograph, be patient, and don't be demanding or pushy. Be polite. Say please and thank you. If you do this, I'm sure anyone will sign for you." No truer words were ever spoken for obtaining autographs than by one of the nicest pro golfers on tour and a very reliable signer. Peter, thank you for your sound advice.

9. If at first you don't succeed, try again! This motto worked for me in getting Senior Tour golfer George Archer's autograph.

10. Last piece of advice: HAVE FUN!

There you have my ten basic tips of getting autographs. Hope these help!

Judy and Peter Jacobsen at
Genoa Lakes Golf Club in Nevada

CHAPTER 15

TOUR OF GOLF ROOM

I've shared many of my prized signatures, but there is more to my collection than just autographed golf balls. Welcome to my golf room, home to one of the largest private collections of golf memorabilia, comprised of hundreds of autographed balls, framed photographs, books, and magazines. This exclusive tour of my golf room offers a pictorial view of many of the cherished golf memorabilia I've accumulated over the past twenty years. The items featured relive some of golf's greatest highlights, such as Tiger Woods reacting to his crucial birdie on the par-3 seventeenth hole at the TPC Stadium Course in Florida in 1994; legend Jack Nicklaus waving good-bye at his last British Open at St Andrews in 2005; and Arnold Palmer on his way to winning in 1964 his fourth Masters with his loyal legion of fans applauding in the background. The gallery of photos is comprised of many memorable moments, showcasing some of the game's great historic events. Granted, my golf room isn't the United States Golf Association (USGA) Museum, home to the world's most extensive collection of golf memorabilia, but it does integrate the treasure of golf memorabilia I've collected since 1989. Each displayed piece in the room has a special place in my heart.

The 1994 U.S. Amateur was all tied up as eighteen-year-old Tiger Woods stepped to the seventeenth tee at the dangerous island green par-3 hole at the TPC at Sawgrass Stadium Course in Ponte Vedra Beach, Florida. TPC at Sawgrass is regarded as one of the toughest golf courses in the world. With the ninety-fourth U.S. Amateur on the line, Tiger was tied with Trip Kuehne after a birdie on the previous hole. Playing at 139 yards, the par-3

Artifacts gracing front wall

Side wall

Hole in One Wall

Back wall

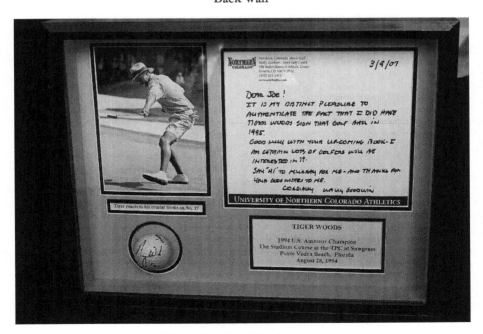

Tiger wins first U.S. Amateur

pin placement was difficult enough to give seasoned professionals nightmares. Taking dead aim, Tiger hit the green, but the ball clung to the fringe, two feet from the water, and fourteen feet from the hole. Facing a sinister and virtually unreadable putt right-to-left downhill, Tiger drained the crucial putt and pumped his fist in celebration as his improbable birdie put him one up in the match. With a final par at 18 to Trip's bogey, Tiger Woods became:

- The first player in history to win both the U.S. Junior and U.S. Amateur championships
- The first African-American U.S. Amateur champion
- The youngest U.S. Amateur in tournament history

The first U.S. Amateur Championship took place in 1895 at Newport Country Club in Newport, Rhode Island, the site where Tiger Woods won his second U.S. Amateur in 1995. He won his third straight Amateur title at Pumpkin Ridge Golf Club located near Portland, Oregon.

Stanford's golf coach, Wally Goodwin, secured Tiger's signature for me on the TCP at Sawgrass logo ball in 1995. Two years later, I asked the Hall of Fame coach to confirm the authenticity of Tiger's signature. Here's the letter he wrote, mounted in the picture frame.

3/9/07
Dear Joe!

It is my distinct pleasure to authenticate the fact that I did have Tiger Woods sign that golf ball in 1995.

Good luck with your upcoming book—I am certain lots of golfers will be interested in it.

Say hi to Murray for me—and thanks for your good wishes to me.

Cordially,
Wally Goodwin

Payne Stewart captures 1999 U.S. Open

You read in Chapter 11 how I acquired Payne Stewart's autograph at Poppy Hill Golf Course in Pebble Beach, in 1991. I'll never forget that unfortunate incident for the rest of my life.

The inscription in the picture frame reads, "Payne Stewart won his first major championship at the 1989 PGA Championship at Kemper Lakes in Illinois, where he entered the final round six strokes back and shot 67 for a one shot margin of victory. Two years later, he captured the 1991 U.S. Open in an eighteen-hole playoff over Scott Simpson, at Hazeltine National Golf Club in Minnesota. Payne's most prolific win came at the 1999 U.S. Open at Pinehurst in North Carolina, sinking a fifteen-foot par putt on the final hole to win by one stroke. Payne one-putted the final three holes in one of the most dramatic finishes in championship history."

Golf Legends

These fifteen autographed golf balls of all-time great legends represent a combined total of 709 PGA and LPGA Tour victories. Here's an individual count of their tour wins, beginning at top left: Ben Hogan (64), Sam Snead (82), Gary Player (24), Tom Watson (39), Byron Nelson (52), Jack Nicklaus (73), Arnold Palmer (62), Kathy Whitworth (88), Gene Sarazen (39), Chi Chi Rodriguez (8), Johnny Miller (25), Ray Floyd (22), Greg Norman (20), Lee Trevino (29), and Mickey Wright (82). All of these legends are in the Golf Hall of Fame.

Hail to the Chiefs

The autographs of the current and former U.S. presidents and special presidential logo balls are shown on top left to right: Richard Nixon, Presidential Seal Ball (unsigned), Gerald Ford, Jimmy Carter, Barack Obama, Ronald Reagan, George H. W. Bush, William Clinton, 1993 President Inauguration logo ball, Jimmy Carter signature Presidential Seal ball (unsigned), and Richard Nixon Library and Birthplace signature ball (unsigned).

Arnie signed vintage Bulls Eye putter

Before I took up golf in 1986, a friend "lent" me an Arnold Palmer signature numbered (8125) Bulls Eye putter in 1978 to play in the weekly Sunday putting contests held at the complex where I lived. I instantly loved the feel of the ball clicking against the familiar flanged-blade, soft brass putter, and played with it very successfully for thirty years until I retired it in 2008. I sent the putter to Arnie to be autographed, and he put on a perfect white-ink signature on the handle. I consider this item to be one of the centerpieces of my golf room.

This signed photo of Arnold Palmer is one of my favorite framed pictures in the room. It's very special to me because Arnie took the time to personalize it for me by handwriting these words.

To Joe,

A Fellow Western Pennsylvanian

Best Wishes

Arnold Palmer

The King

Tom Lehman Drains $100,000 Putt

I mentioned in Chapter 2 that my wife and I attended the 1997 Skins Game, played at the new Rancho La Quinta Country Club in the La Quinta, California. On the first day of the match, we witnessed PGA Tour pro Tom Lehman win $100,000 on a single carry-over hole, draining an eighteen-foot birdie on the par-3 eighth hole to take the lead over Tiger Woods (1996 PGA Tour Player of the Year), Mark O'Meara (fourteen-time PGA Tour winner) and David Duval, a late replacement for defending champion, Fred Couples.

Tom won another $30,000 on the ninth hole and ended up winning the Skins Game, earning $300,000—not bad for two days of play. Tom signed the photo for me at Pebble Beach the following year.

Lee Janzen claims second U.S. Open at Olympic Club

PGA Tour pro Lee Janzen began Sunday, June 21, 1998, with two early bogeys that put him seven shots behind Payne Stewart. Seven strokes behind with fifteen holes to play are similar to down five runs in the bottom of the ninth, with one out and nobody on base. The fifth hole presented a stroke of bad and good luck. Lee pushed a 4-wood off the tee into the trees. Lee looked everywhere for the ball and was told by a spectator that the ball never fell down. After several minutes of looking for the ball, Lee formally gave up. In an interview afterward, he commented, "I started walking back to the tee thinking I had to play very well just to make a double-bogey on the hole." As he returned to the tee to hit what would have been his third shot, someone yelled the ball had just dropped into the rough. He ended up saving par on No. 5 and made some splendid shots down the stretch to end the day shooting a 2-under-par 68 to finish at exactly even-par 280 and beat Payne Stewart by a stroke, in a rematch of their final-round duel in 1993 at Baltusrol Golf Club in New Jersey. Janzen was the only golfer to record par in the 1998 U.S. Open.

His final-round comeback was one for the books. Besides winning $535,000, Lee also won on Father's Day, with both his father and son in attendance.

I bought the photo from Taylor Made, Janzen's sponsor, and was able to get him to sign it at Pebble Beach. The ball in the framed picture is the official logo golf ball of the 1998 U.S. Open at the Olympic Club in San Francisco.

The Associated Press Collection
Augusta National Golf Club
Arnold Palmer
1960 Masters

Masters victory No. 4 for Arnie

The man who added "Charge" to our golf wordbook watches the flight of his fairway iron shot en route to winning his fourth Masters in 1964, thus becoming the first player to win the Masters four times.

The large, framed black-and-white photo came from the exclusive Associated Press Collection, comprised of photos of some of the greatest golfers in the history of the game. Arnie was kind enough to autograph the collectible fourteen-by-eighteen inch photograph for my private collection.

Jack waves good-bye at St. Andrews

Jack Nicklaus is seen in the photo waving good-bye to the appreciative crowd from the historic Swilcan Bridge. An awesome piece of memorabilia, I was fortunate to have my brother-in-law, Rex Patterson, get Jack to personally sign the picture, in 2006, with the help of the head pro at Bayside Resort Golf Club, Delaware's first Jack Nicklaus Signature Golf Course. I bought the framed piece on eBay and sent the photo to Rex, who lives at Bayside.

How important is the name of Jack Nicklaus? His name in Scotland practically rivals the royal family. The Royal and Ancient Club of St. Andrews changed the British Open site in 2005 to the Home of Golf, the Old Course at St. Andrews, in order to accommodate the three-time British Open Champion's emotional desire to play his last major championship on the world golf stage.

To commemorate his retirement after competing in his thirty-seventh British Open Championship and his two Open wins at St. Andrews, in 1970 and 1978, the Royal Bank of Scotland issued a limited five-pound note honoring Jack Nicklaus in his last Open competition as a professional golfer. The bank issued only two million of the banknotes, now sold-out. The uncirculated note is dated 14 July 2005, the last time Jack competed at St. Andrews. Jack is the first living person outside of the royal family to actually be featured on a banknote. These commemorative five-pound notes with his image featured on the front of the note are much sought-after by collectors. My signed photo, with bank note and all, is a collector's dream.

Jack's last putt in the British Open, the oldest tournament in golf, is a storybook finish. With thousands of fans lining the eighteenth fairway and surrounding the green, Jack raised his putter in triumph as his final breaking putt of about thirteen feet dropped in for a spectacular birdie, with the crowd erupting into a roar, reverberating throughout the golf course. The greatest golfer of all time received a ten-minute standing ovation.

The Golden Bear's last round at St. Andrews was a magical and fitting moment in golf history.

"Farewell to St. Andrews"

Most golfers know that the Old Course at St. Andrews in Scotland is where golf began. For some professional golfers, e.g., Arnold Palmer and Jack Nicklaus, their remarkable careers ended in grand fashion at the Old Course.

Two-time British Open Champion (1961 and 1962) Arnold Palmer, made his thirty-fifth and final appearance at St. Andrews during the 1995 Open. Arnie is pictured bidding his legions farewell from the Swilcan Bridge on the storied eighteenth hole, thus closing the curtains on one of the most phenomenal careers in golf.

I truly believe that Arnold Palmer will go down in golf history as the most beloved professional golfer. I openly want to thank him for not only personally hand-signing "Farewell to St. Andrews," but also for autographing nineteen other golf-related items on display in my golf room.

One of five racks displaying signed balls

In the twenty years since the creation of the golf room, my memorabilia collection has grown to more than 260 prized golf pieces, which must be seen to be truly appreciated. The room sparks conversations when friends come to visit. One of the questions people ask me most often is, "What is your collection worth?" I reply, "I really don't know nor do I care. None of my cherished golf possessions are for sale for any price." The real value of my collection lies in all the thrills and memories I have of acquiring the autographed items. These fond memories will last a lifetime.

CHAPTER 16

THE 19TH HOLE: REVIEWING THE ROUND

As a longtime collector, avid golf reader and website researcher, I've absorbed an amazing amount of golf knowledge as I've pursued my hobby. I rediscovered the joy of collecting after losing interest later in my teenage years. I've made many new friends and connections that would not have occurred if the collecting bug hadn't grabbed me once again. It's been a thrill to track down celebrities for their autographs and take comfort in ownership of my vast private collection.

As golf is "addictive," so is collecting autographs. The better you become at both, the more you want to play and collect. At seventy-four years of age, I am caught up in the suspense and excitement of the hunt itself and the thrill of the conquest in meeting famous people and having balls personally signed. I am proud to say that my collection continues to grow to this day. It's been a journey that has practically turned into my life's work.

For the many golf tournaments I've attended, the hundreds of days I spent chasing down celebrities, and the countless hours I waited patiently in line to get those special autographs, I can honestly say that the fruits of my labor and dedication paid off. For my untiring efforts, I claim to have one of the largest private collection of autographed golf balls in the country, in my very own golf room! I never tire of viewing all the prized golf memorabilia and showing off the collection to friends. I plan to continue acquiring autographs as long as the journey remains exhilarating and fun.

Today, hundreds of fans continuously line up at pro golfing events such as the Bob Hope Chrysler Classic, AT&T Pebble Beach National Pro-Am, Frank Sinatra Celebrity Invitational, American Century Championship, and many LPGA events to obtain sought-after signatures from their favorite players and celebrities. Autograph fans will continue to multiply for years to come as the game of golf gains popularity. Tiger Woods, golf's biggest star, has made it "cool" to play golf now and for future generations. His popularity has brought golf galleries to a new level. Also motivating young golfers is the current No. 1 ranked women's professional golfer in the world, Lorena Ochoa. This magnetic and charming top Mexican golfing star continues to attract a huge fan base wherever she plays. The debut of highly touted Michelle Wie in 2009 as a full-fledged LPGA tour member creates new enthusiasm as well. She's regarded as the most interesting player to watch on tour. Wie's sheer athleticism and strength will attract young people and their families to watch the lengthy drives that have made her game famous. As popularity of golf's top stars grows, so will the demand increase for their signatures and endorsements.

I now can finally understand why autograph collecting is such an exciting pastime and a rewarding journey. Owning the autograph of a golf legend like Arnold Palmer holds enormous sentimental value and has given me so much pleasure in knowing that the most popular golfer of all time autographed twenty items displayed in my golf room.

A close friend asked, "Since your golf autograph collection grows practically by the week, will there be a sequel to your book?" I replied, "I don't think so. Writing this book was much harder than I realized, but I have to say that authoring *Hooked on Autographs* was a challenge and a once-in-a-lifetime adventure for me." This book was created purely out of love for the game of golf and the rewarding thrill of collecting autographs from so many famous superstars, who hail from all walks of life.

Although I plan to continue my quest for collecting famous signatures, I probably will never cross paths again with the likes of Arnold Palmer, Sammy Snead, Chi Chi Rodriquez, Jack Lemmon, Jack Nicklaus, Gary Player, Bob Hope, Lee Trevino, and all the other beloved golf legends whose greatness, unique personalities and captivating stories made this book possible. These pioneers and true legends were forged from a different mold. Their legacy will last forever.

An inspirational quote by legendary Arnold Palmer motivated me to keep focused in order to fulfill my dream of completing my first book: "The most rewarding things you do in life are often the ones that look like they cannot be done."

I hope *Hooked on Autographs* is a fitting compliment to the personalities and significant achievements of the celebrities featured here. I also hope that potential collectors will draw inspiration and encouragement from the pages within. After all these years, collecting famous autographs still excites me to no end.

Joe Galiardi

A percentage of the author's royalties from this book will go to the Walter Reed Society, a tax-exempt charitable organization established, among other things, to ease family burdens and speed healing for the returning wounded soldiers from Iraq and Afghanistan, many of whom are on the brink of financial disaster. The soldiers, who made great sacrifices in the line of duty, will truly appreciate your donation. Whatever the amount you give—no matter how large or small—will be greatly appreciated by those who sacrificed so much for us. Send your tax-deductible contribution to:

Walter Reed Society, Inc.
P.O. Box 59611
Walter Reed Station
Washington, DC 20012-9611

Made in the USA